James Gee 74

Pelican Books
Marx in His Own Words

Ernst Fischer was born in Austria in 1889. He studied philosophy at Graz, and did unskilled work in a factory. In 1927 he joined the staff of *Arbeiter-Zeitung*, and remained there until 1934. Having helped to initiate left-wing opposition within the Social Democratic Party he became a member of the Communist Party. In 1945 he took part in the establishment of a provincial government in Austria, where he was for a short time Minister of Education. He founded and was chief editor of *Neues Osterreich*, but since 1959 has confined himself to the literary field, writing many books and plays. *The Necessity of Art* was published by Penguins in 1963; *Art Against Ideology* (1969), *Marx in His Own Words* (1970) and *Lenin in His Own Words* (1972), the latter two in collaboration with Franz Marek, were published by Allen Lane The Penguin Press. He died in 1972.

D0715933

Marx
in His Own Words

ERNST FISCHER
IN COLLABORATION
WITH
FRANZ MAREK

TRANSLATED BY
ANNA BOSTOCK

PENGUIN BOOKS

Penguin Books Ltd, Harmondsworth, Middlesex, England
Penguin Books Australia Ltd, Ringwood, Victoria, Australia

Was Marx Wirklich sagte first published in Vienna by Verlag Fritz Molden 1968
This translation published by Allen Lane The Penguin Press 1970
Published in Pelican Books 1973
Copyright © Verlag Fritz Molden, 1968
Translation copyright © Anna Bostock, 1970

Made and Printed in Great Britain by
Cox & Wyman Ltd, London, Reading and Fakenham
Set in Monotype Plantin

This book is sold subject to the condition that
it shall not, by way of trade or otherwise, be lent,
re-sold, hired out, or otherwise circulated without
the publisher's prior consent in any form of
binding or cover other than that in which it is
published and without a similar condition
including this condition being imposed on the
subsequent purchaser

CONTENTS

BIOGRAPHICAL DATA

1818   5 May: Karl Heinrich Marx born at Trier, the son of Heinrich Marx, a solicitor. His father, the offspring of an old family of Rabbis, had adopted Christianity a year previously.

1830–35   After a childhood spent in an atmosphere of prosperity and culture, Karl Marx attends the Jesuit grammar school at Trier for a period of five years. His intellectual development is encouraged, not so much by the school, as by his father – who has a lively interest in philosophy – and by State Councillor Ludwig von Westphalen, with whom he reads the Greek poets and Shakespeare.

1835–41   Attends Bonn University and, after two terms, Berlin University, where he reads jurisprudence, philosophy and history. As a student Marx makes excerpts from Aristotle, Spinoza, Leibniz, Hume and Kant, and writes some romantic poems, a fragment of a tragedy and a few chapters of a novel in the manner of Laurence Sterne. In 1836 he becomes engaged to Jenny von Westphalen, his older friend's daughter. Increasingly influenced by Hegel's philosophy, which he at first dismisses as 'grotesque craggy melody'. Clashes with his father, who is alarmed by K.M.'s passionate nature, lack of moderation and financial insouciance.

1838   Father dies on 10 May.

1841   Doctor's degree awarded in recognition of a thesis on Democritus and Epicurus.

1842   Joins staff of liberal paper *Rheinische Zeitung*. Becomes editor-in-chief on 15 October.

1843   18 March: leaves the paper on account of increasing difficulties with the censorship office. Marries Jenny von Westphalen on 12 June. Moves to Paris at the end of October; edits radical *Deutsch–Französische Jahr-bücher* together with Arnold Ruge.
Start of close collaboration with Frederick Engels, the son of a manufacturer of Barmen, two years younger than K.M. Contacts with Heinrich Heine, French socialists and the proletatiat. *Economic and Political Manuscripts*.

1845   Expelled from France at the demand of the Prussian government. Moves to Brussels. *The Holy Family*. Financial troubles, which are to persist until the end of his life.

1846   *The German Ideology*, on which K.M. had begun work at the end of 1845. *Theses on Feuerbach*. Contacts with the English Chartists and the 'League of the Just' (via a communist correspondence bureau).

1847   *The Poverty of Philosophy*. Debate with Proud'hon. Collaboration with the 'Communist League'. Participation in the second congress of the League, held in London.

1848   February: *Manifesto of the Communist Party*. Revolution in France. In early March, expulsion from Brussels. Revolutions in Germany, Hungary and Austria. Marx and Engels in Cologne. On 31st May first issue of the *Neue Rheinische Zeitung* with Marx as editor-in-chief. Dissolution of the Communist League.

1849   Marx is accused of incitement to armed rebellion but acquitted by a Cologne jury. On 16 May, after the triumph of the counter-revolution, he is expelled as a 'stateless' person. The last issue of the *Neue Rheinische Zeitung* appears on 18 May. Arrival in Paris, 3 June; beginning of exile in London, 24 August.

1850   *The Class Struggles in France.* Re-founding of the Communist League. *Neue Rheinische Zeitung. Politisch-Ökonomische Revue* is launched, but has to cease publication after five issues. Split in the League.

1851   Begins contributing to *New York Tribune*.

1852   *The Eighteenth Brumaire of Louis Bonaparte.* October and November: trial of communists in Cologne. Seven of the accused are condemned to life imprisonment in a fortress. Final dissolution of the League.

1853   *Revelations About the Cologne Communist Trial.*

1855-62 Writes hundreds of articles for *New York Tribune, Neue Oder-Zeitung,* Urquhart's *Free Press,* Jones's *People's Paper* and *Wiener Presse.* Constant poverty and ill-health. Jenny Marx suffers nervous breakdowns. Engels gives continual assistance.

1859   *A Contribution to The Critique of Political Economy.* Political differences with Ferdinand Lassalle, with whom Marx has been acquainted since 1848. Lassalle's view that the liberal bourgeoisie, rather than the reactionary Junkers, are the principal enemy becomes increasingly the main subject of disagreement.

1860   The pamphlet *Herr Vogt*.

1861   Marx and Lassalle meet in Berlin.

1863   Lassalle's agitational and organizational activities in Germany reach their climax.

1864   31 August: Lassalle dies following a duel. 28 September: founding of the First International in London. Union of all tendencies within the labour movement – trade unionists, communists, socialists, anarchists. Marx is elected as one of the thirty-two members of the General Council. The programme outlined in his inaugural address is unanimously adopted.

1865   Break with the General Union of German Workers founded by Lassalle and directed after his death by Johann Baptist von Schweitzer. Conference of the International in London. *Wages, Price, Profit.*

1866   First Congress of the International in Geneva.

1867   *Capital*, Vol. I. Second Congress of the International in Lausanne.

1868   Third Congress of the International in Basle.

1869   Fourth Congress of the International in Basle. Open clash between Marx and Michael Bakunin, the theoretician of anarchism and leader of the 'International Alliance of Socialist Democrats'; however, no decision is reached. Congress of the German Social-Democratic Workers' Party at Eisenach.

1870   Franco-German War. *Addresses of the General Council of the International*. Engels moves to London.

1871   The Paris Commune. *The Civil War in France*. Conference of the International in London.

1872   Last Congress of the International at The Hague. Expulsion of Bakunin.

1875   Unification congress of the German workers' parties at Gotha. Founding of the Social-Democratic Workers' Party. *A Critique of the Gotha Programme.*

1878   The Social-Democratic Party banned in Germany.

1881   Death of Jenny Marx on 2 December.

1883   Death of Karl Marx on 14 March.

1885   *Capital*, Vol. II, edited by Frederick Engels.

1894   *Capital*, Vol. III, edited by Frederick Engels.

AUTHOR'S FOREWORD

To select what is essential from the vast body of Karl Marx's work – philosophy, political economy, anthropology, social criticism, history, theory of revolutionary practice, visions of the future – and to comment on these essentials, all in the space of barely two hundred pages, under the ambitious title of *Marx in His Own Words*, is a bold undertaking indeed. My friend Franz Marek and I, working in collaboration, have attempted to carry it out. Marx *really said* every word of the texts we quote: but, should anyone point out that he said a great deal more besides, we should be the first to agree. He did say a great deal more, and he made great demands upon his readers. With the exception of a few texts he is not an easy author to read. My collaborator and I were faced over and over again with the question: how much may we expect from our readers without making them lose heart? How much may we simplify without injury to Marx's greatness and originality? We have presupposed an intelligent reader – yourself – and we have endeavoured, for your information, to put the *real* Marx against the distorted image so often presented of him.

Marx the revolutionary thinker, Marx the man was far from being an infallible Father of any Church, a cold analyst or an advocate of violence.

Filled to the brim with the 'principle of greatness', he combined vision with science, philosophy with practice, theory with action – passionately, radically, intolerantly: a man who set out not merely to interpret the world but to change it, and whose ideas have gripped millions of human beings and are still shaking the world.

We have chosen to let Marx speak for himself. Our comments are confined to pointing out certain connexions, rendering comprehension easier, separating what is permanent from what was time-conditioned and has been overtaken by historical development – that is to say, applying the critical method of Marxism to Marxism itself.

The reader we visualize has an open mind. He has had enough of propaganda of every kind, and wishes only to be informed.

I

THE DREAM OF THE
WHOLE MAN

Marx's thought underwent many variations in the course of his life, but what had served as his starting point remained intact: the possibility of the whole, the *total* man.

Since the triumph of the industrial revolution and of the capitalist method of production at the turn of the eighteenth century, the fragmentation of man through the division of labour, mechanization, exploitation and commerce had become the fundamental European experience. The longing for unity with one's own self, with one's kind and with nature, from which man had become alienated, was common to all those who entertained humanist feelings and ideas.

In their romantic revolt against a world which turned everything into a commodity and degraded man to the status of an object, the poets and philosophers of the iron age complained that man had become a fragment of his own self, had been overpowered by his own works, had fallen away from himself.

Enjoyment was divorced from labour, the means from the end, the effort from the reward. Everlastingly chained to a single little fragment of the Whole, man himself develops into nothing but a fragment; everlastingly in his ear the monotonous sound of the wheel that he turns, he never develops the harmony of his being, and instead of putting the stamp of humanity upon his own nature, he becomes nothing more than the imprint of his occupation or of his specialized knowledge. (Friedrich Schiller: *On the Aesthetic Education of Man, in a Series of Letters.* Trans.

Elizabeth M. Wilkinson and L. A. Willoughby. Clarendon Press, Oxford, 1967. Sixth letter, p. 35.)

The age of turbulent development of technology and industry, of greed and the mercantile spirit, of capital and of proletarian misery, of revolutionary hopes and their disappointment by post-revolutionary reality, became the age of romantic protest against the complacent bourgeoisie. Both the aristocratic and the plebeian opponents of the bourgeois world joined in that protest; both condemned the dehumanization of man by the progressive division of labour whose extreme consequence, at one end of society, was ever-increasing wealth and, at the other, ever-increasing material and spiritual wretchedness. But, as time went on, a certain differentiation took place within the romantic movement: some looked to the past as the only mainspring of salvation and imagined it as a time of human unity and dignity; others turned towards the future, dreaming of the resurgence of the whole man in a coming realm of freedom, abundance and humanity.

The political revolutions in America and France had proclaimed man's right to liberty – the 'free personality'. The contrast between such proclamations and the reality which followed was painful to many. Man in bourgeois society had indeed become an individual – not in community with others, but in harsh competition against them. 'Liberty as a right of man', wrote the young Marx, 'is not founded upon the relations between man and man, but rather upon the separation of man from man.'[1]

None of the supposed rights of man, therefore, go beyond the egoistic man, man as he is, as a member of civil society; that is, an individual separated from the community, withdrawn into himself, wholly preoccupied with his private interest and acting in accordance with his private caprice.[2]

The problem therefore was to turn men, reduced to an empty

individuality, away from purely private interests and pre-occupations, to unite the individual with a community based on the freedom of all rather than on the dominance of a few.

The notes Marx made for his doctoral thesis at Berlin University at the age of twenty-one do not as yet contain any mention of the class struggle, of the proletariat and revolution, of the 'realm of freedom' in a classless society without rulers. But we do find, in the sixth notebook, the following sentence on the subjectivism, the fundamental self-centredness of the epicurean and stoical philosophies: 'Thus, when the universal sun has set, does the moth seek the lamp-light of privacy.' And even earlier, in the third notebook: 'He who no longer finds pleasure in building the whole world with his own forces, in being a world-creator instead of revolving forever inside his own skin, on him the Spirit has spoken its anathema.' And finally, in the seventh notebook: 'Least of all are we entitled to assume, on the strength of authority and good faith, that a philosophy is a philosophy, even if the authority is that of a whole nation and the faith is that of centuries.'[3]

The 'universal sun' for Marx was the individual's commitment to a common goal, his participation in the *res publica*, the public cause, the fact that his actions and ideas can transcend narrow private interest – in other words, something like Athenian democracy or the Roman republic before the dictatorship of the Caesars. Marx refused to 'revolve forever inside his own skin': he wanted to be a 'world-creator', making the world intellectually his own and eventually contributing to its material transformation. The desire for a new social dawn, for a 'universal' sun that would make the lamplight of privacy appear dull by comparison, is unmistakable. But equally there is the stirring of a critical mind unprepared to accept authority and good faith as proof of the truth of any philosophy, doctrine or system. Marx at twenty-one was already eager to forge ahead towards a new universality, to be the creator of a new world – without forgoing the right to submit everything already in existence, or coming into existence, to critical re-examination.

In Berlin, where Marx read jurisprudence, philosophy and history, the dominant spirit was that of Hegel, who exercised a great fascination over the younger scholars and thinkers. In his gigantic philosophical opus, which was both the crowning point and the negation of romanticism, Hegel saw the world spirit in world history traverse every successive form of alienation – of the falling away from the self – and simultaneously also of the return to the self, of reconciliation, thus progressing from an unconscious unity with the self to a conscious one. Hegel's difficult philosophy was a manifestation of the contradictory dynamic of his age – the notion of development, the dream of a realm of freedom and plenitude, of a reality that has become conscious of itself.

Marx as a young man at first rejected Hegel, but was soon captivated by the great philosopher and his dialectic. He was to remain faithful to the dialectic – the inner contradiction within the nature of thought and of all things, the recognition that nothing can be understood in isolation or as a rectilinear sequence of cause and effect, but only as the multiple interaction of all factors and as being in conflict with itself: that everything, as it comes into being, produces its own negation and tends to progress towards the negation of the negation. But he went far beyond Hegel in the consequences he drew.

As editor of the liberal *Rheinische Zeitung* in 1842–3, Marx with his radical-democratic views became a thorn in the flesh of the Germany of the 1840s and had to move to Paris. Writing in the *Deutsch–Französische Jahrbücher* in 1844, he described and castigated the conditions in Germany from which he had escaped in the following words:

German history, indeed, prides itself upon a development which no other nation had previously accomplished, or will ever imitate in the historical sphere. We have shared in the restorations of modern nations without ever sharing in their revolutions. We have been restored, first because other nations have dared to make revolutions, and secondly because other nations have suffered counter-revolutions; in the first case because our masters were afraid, and in the second case because they were not afraid. Led by our shepherds, we have only once kept company with liberty and that was on the day of its interment.[4]

In Paris Marx met the young Frederick Engels, the son of a manufacturer from the Rhineland, then working in London. Through him he not only gained an insight into the social conditions prevailing in the most advanced industrial country of the time, but, above all, Engels became a friend such as there have been only few in history. During the collaboration which followed and which was unparalleled in its closeness and in the length of its duration, Engels recognized – without a trace of envy – the surpassing genius of his occasionally somewhat difficult friend, and became his devoted helper not only in intellectual, scientific and political matters but also, over and over again, in private life. Engels's philosophical contribution to Marxism can be contested: but the productive and enduring friendship which united Marx and Engels stands high above all criticism.

What Marx came to know in Paris was the proletariat.

He saw the wretched figure of the proletarian as the quintessence of dehumanization, the extreme of everything the Romantics felt to be the denial and mockery of the nature of man. But precisely in this extreme negation Marx saw the hope of overcoming it. He believed that the proletariat was forced by its very poverty to liberate itself from inhuman conditions by overturning those conditions at their base, and that, by liberating itself, it would become the liberator of mankind.

There is an extraordinary poignancy about the way Marx

described the negation of man as found in the proletarian of his time.

Labour certainly produces marvels for the rich, but it produces privation for the worker. It produces palaces, but hovels for the worker. It produces beauty, but deformity for the worker. It replaces labour by machinery, but it casts some of the workers back into a barbarous kind of work and turns the others into machines. It produces intelligence, but also stupidity and cretinism for the workers.[5]

The proletarian in his work does not fulfil himself but denies himself,

has a feeling of misery rather than well-being, does not develop freely his mental and physical energies but is physically exhausted and mentally debased. The worker therefore feels himself at home only during his leisure time, whereas at work he feels homeless.[6]

Marx was, of course, a master of needle-sharp comment, but many contemporary records prove that he was not exaggerating when he spoke of the wretchedness of the proletarian. The Young Hegelians, the great philosopher's radical disciples, expected atheism to liberate man by bringing his spirit back from the beyond into the real world. Marx's view was more profound; the criticism of religion was for him 'the premise of all criticism', but he was aware of the need for liberation from material as well as spiritual bondage, and he saw religion both as 'the expression of real misery' and as the 'protest against real misery'. 'Religion is the sigh of the oppressed creature, the sentiment of a heartless world, and the soul of soulless conditions. It is the *opium* of the people.'[7] As is so often the case, not many people are aware of what Marx really said in this context: the quotation is usually twisted to imply that religion was opium *for* the people, that is to say a narcotic given the people by outside forces, while the preceding sentence is ignored.

Atheism, as a denial of this unreality [the unreality of man and nature], is no longer meaningful, for atheism is a *negation of God* and seeks to assert by this negation the *existence of man*. Socialism no longer requires such a roundabout method; it begins from the *theoretical* and *practical sense perception* of man and nature as essential beings. It is positive human *self-consciousness*, no longer a self-consciousness attained through the negation of religion; just as the *real life* of man is positive and no longer attained through the negation of private property, through communism. . . . Communism is the necessary form and the dynamic principle of the immediate future, but communism is not itself the goal of human development – the form of human society.[8]

We can see that religion, atheism and communism were, for Marx, stages or features of development rather than its goal. The goal was positive humanism, the real life of man. The existence of the proletariat was the most striking contradiction of such a life; but 'the ruptured reality of industry' did not manifest itself in the proletariat alone. Scientific analysis of capitalist industry confirmed a hundred times over what Schiller had only apprehended: that 'enjoyment was divorced from labour, the means from the end, the effort from the reward'; that the proletarian was only the most extreme expression of the fragmentary, disconnected, rent nature of the world of machines, profits and poverty. As the negation became more clearly pronounced, so the thing it negated became clearer too: the unrealized image of man.

The starting point of religion is God. Hegel's starting point was the State. Marx's was Man.

In the *Critique of Hegel's State Law* Marx wrote:

Hegel proceeds from the State and makes man the State subjectified; democracy proceeds from man and makes the State man objectified . . .

Man does not exist for law's sake, law exists for man's sake; it is *human existence*, whereas [for] the others man is *legal existence*. That is the fundamental difference of democracy.[9]

The decisive thing for Marx is not simply 'the universal', a system as an end in itself, but man – concrete, real, individual man. The object of his thinking, of all his efforts, is the whole man, the reality of man, positive humanism.

Man needs the community in order to develop into a free individual. 'In the previous substitutes for the community, in the State, etc., personal freedom has existed only for the individuals who developed within the relationships of this ruling class, and only in so far as they were individuals of the class.' Individuals who behave as though they were independent are in actual fact conditioned not only by the whole of social development – by language, tradition, upbringing, etc. – but also by their class, estate or profession. Their personality is conditioned and determined by quite definite class relationships. Although the mutual relationship between them is a relationship between persons, it is above all one between 'social character masks' – not as specific individuals, but as standardized 'average individuals'. Marx hoped and believed that with the 'community of revolutionary proletarians' it would be just the reverse: individuals would participate in it as individuals. Marx saw communism, and, with it, common control over the conditions which 'were previously abandoned to chance and had won an independent existence over against the separate individuals just because of their separation as individuals',[10] not as a system of classes and castes – of 'social character masks' – but as a free association of individual men.

Between the individual and society there is an interaction:

As society itself produces *man* as *man*, so it is *produced* by him. . . . The *human* significance of nature only exists for *social* man, because only in this case is nature a *bond* with other *men*, the basis of his existence for others and of their existence for him.

Only then is nature the *basis* of his own *human* experience and a vital element of human reality.[11]

Although our time of scientific and technical revolution calls for an ever-increasing measure of team-work, the work of a scholar, a writer or an artist is not *directly* bound up with other people and may actually suffer from direct social intervention. Yet such work presupposes a community with others; it draws on the experience of others, it is essentially a form of social activity despite all its autonomy.

It is not only the material of my activity – such as the language itself which the thinker uses – which is given to me as a social product. My *own existence* is a social activity. For this reason, what I myself produce I produce for society, and with the consciousness of acting as a social being.[12]

This is not flat utilitarianism, not just a matter of one's activity being of direct use to society. The point here is the social nature of the individual – *the personality as the outcome and justification of society*.

Though man is a unique individual – and it is just his particularity which makes him an individual, a really *individual* communal being – he is equally the *whole*, the ideal whole, the subjective existence of society as thought and experienced. He exists in reality as the representation and the real mind of social existence, and as the sum of human manifestations of life.[13]

This totality of man proclaimed by Marx, this 'humanity in man's nature' as Schiller called it, is at first only an idea, only (but for a few exceptions) a possibility as yet unrealized. Fragmentary, imperfect, disfigured man is incapable of transforming himself into total man; he can only do so through society as it develops. The more a man is able to take possession of the outside world – through his senses, his spirit, his intelligence – and the more integrated and many-sided this taking of possession, this 'appropriation' is, the greater is his chance of becoming a *whole* man.

Man appropriates his manifold being in an all-inclusive way, and thus as a whole man. All his *human* relations to the world – seeing, hearing, smelling, tasting, touching, thinking, observing, feeling, desiring, acting, loving – in short, all the organs of his individuality, like the organs which are directly communal in form, are in their objective action (their *action in relation to the object*) an appropriation of this object, the appropriation of human reality. The way in which they react to the object is the confirmation of *human reality*. It is human effectiveness and human suffering, for suffering humanly considered is an enjoyment of the self for man.[14]

The objects which man makes his own through his senses, his intellect and his imagination become his own objectification: he unites with them, makes them his own creation and part of his own self by absorbing them. The whole development of the human race is needed in order to humanize the senses and to educate them so that they became *human* senses.

Many commentators overlooked the fact that when Marx speaks of this 'all-inclusive' appropriation and of the 'man endowed with all the senses', he in fact means a creative act, an artistic act in the broadest sense of that term: that, for Marx, love was an essential form of such 'appropriation'. In a world of possession, of commerce and profit, this humane act has shrivelled into the mere act of *having*. Marx speaks with passion against the mentality of *having*, which sees immediate, physical possession as 'the unique goal of life and existence'.[15] This mentality has infected love itself, twisting the relationship between man and woman into a relationship of ownership and domination; marriage in its present form – 'a form of exclusive private property' – and the demand of a 'crude and unreflective communism' for the common ownership of women are both concerned with *appropriation through having* and therefore mean man's debasement and reduction to a *thing*.

In the relationship with *woman*, as the prey and the handmaid of communal lust, is expressed the infinite degradation in which man exists for himself. . . . From this relationship man's whole level of development can be assessed. It follows from the character of this relationship how far *man* has become, and has understood himself as, a *species-being*, a *human* being. The relationship of man to woman is the *most natural* relation of human being to human being. It indicates, therefore, how far man's *natural* behaviour has become *human*, and how far his *human* essence has become a *natural* essence for him, how far his *human nature* has become *nature* for him. It also shows how far man's needs have become *human* needs, and consequently how far the other person, as a person, has become one of his needs, and to what extent he is in his individual existence at the same time a social being.[16]

The most natural relationship thus becomes a measure of humanization: the development from faceless sexuality to 'higher sexual union' (as Goethe called it), a community of the senses, the spirit and the mind, a recognition of the other as a fellow being, does not destroy nature but enhances it until it becomes true *human nature*. In 1843 Marx married a beautiful bride, Jenny von Westphalen. On 21 June 1856 he wrote his wife a letter from London in which he said:

Momentary absence is good, for present things appear too alike for us to distinguish them. Even towers when they are close seem dwarfish, whereas small everyday things, when they are close, loom far too large. Small habits which assume the form of passions when they are close to us, disappear as soon as their immediate object is out of sight. Great passions which, because of the proximity of their object, take on the form of small habits, grow and reassume their natural dimensions by the magic effect of distance. Thus it is with my love. You only need to be removed from me – if only by dreams – and I know at once that time does to my love for you what sun and rain do to a plant: it makes it grow. My love for you, as soon as you are far away, appears as what it is, a giant wherein all the energy of my mind and all the character of my heart is concentrated. I feel a man once more because I feel a great passion. The complexities in which study and modern education involve us, the scepticism we must necessarily bring to bear on all subjective and objective impressions, are perfectly designed to make all of us small and weak and petulant and undecided. But love, not the love of Feuerbach's Man nor Moleschott's metabolism, nor again love of the Proletariat, but love of the beloved and more particularly of you, makes a man a man again . . .

'Buried in her arms, revived by her kisses' – yes, in your arms and by your kisses – and the Brahmins and Pythagoras can keep their doctrine of reincarnation for all I care, and Christianity its teaching of the Resurrection.[17]

Thus, by appropriation through love, nature has become human nature.

Man educates himself to be a man by humanizing his nature, by refusing to degrade other men into objects but, instead, by making the objects of nature his own – humanly apprehended, recognized, formed objects by means of whose human appropriation he develops the wealth of his capabilities and the plenitude of his own self. Appropriation by having, fragmentation of potential plenitude into a patchwork of private property, makes man 'stupid and partial'. Yet appropriation by possession has been and still is the inevitable step towards a fully productive society in which demands grow in step with capacities and man is not degraded to an object – in other words, a truly human society.

Marx was not a lachrymose moral preacher. While revealing the monstrous nature of appropriation through having, of the rule of private ownership and the dehumanization of man through the capitalist method of production he recognized it to be a necessary phase of historical development and saw a new reality ripening within it.

Private property has made us so stupid and partial that an object is only *ours* when we have it, when it exists for us as capital or when it is directly eaten, drunk, worn, inhabited, etc., in short *utilized* in some way . . .

Thus *all* the physical and intellectual senses have been replaced by the simple alienation of *all* these senses; the sense of *having*. The human being had to be reduced to this absolute poverty in order to be able to give birth to all his inner wealth.[18]

A sense that is cramped by crude practical necessity is bound to be a sadly limited one. To a starving man, it matters little whether food is presented in a form fit for human consumption or not: he cares only for its abstract existence as food. 'It could just as well exist in the most crude form, and it is impossible to say in what this feeding-activity would differ from that of animals.'[19]

What does this mean? It means that there must be no more starving people, that society must not only become capable of satisfying the most primitive requirements but must advance towards higher, more differentiated needs – needs which are no longer animal but human. The material for such a future is accumulated in the society of private ownership.

Just as society at its beginnings finds, through the development of *private property* with its wealth and poverty (both intellectual and material), the materials necessary for this *cultural development*, so fully constituted society produces man in all the plenitude of his being, the wealthy man endowed with all the senses, as an enduring reality.[20]

Marx saw bourgeois society with all its contradictions as a society *in the process of becoming*. He dreamed of communism as a society that had completed this process. He did not expect communism to be the simple negation of private property but its positive abolition in a world of plenty, of humanity and integrated intelligence: 'the real appropriation of human nature through and for man.'[21]

Communism as Marx anticipated it was 'the *definitive* resolution of the antagonism between man and nature, and

27

between man and man'. He hoped that communism would mean the transformation of 'naturalism' (that is to say the premises supplied by nature) into 'humanism' (that is to say the full flowering of total, conscious and no longer divided man). Both in his youth and at the end of his life Marx's aim was not the deadening but the humanizing of the senses; not the replacement of the body by the mind or *vice versa* but the development of all capacities for production or enjoyment; not material or spiritual impoverishment but all-round appropriation of the world and all its possibilities; not standardization and depersonalization but the manifold nature of individuality living in a free community with others.

Did Marx, then, see communism as a final state, an elysium, a paradise? On the contrary: for him it meant the mere beginning of true human development. Dreams always precede reality. Thought precedes action.

In order to supersede the *idea* of private property communist *ideas* are sufficient, but genuine communist activity is necessary in order to supersede *real* private property. History will produce it, and the development which we already recognize in thought as self-transcending will in reality involve a severe and protracted process. We must consider it an advance, however, that we have previously acquired an awareness of the limited nature and the goal of the historical development and can see beyond it.[22]

Consciousness, then, goes farther than the goal and farther than the limitations of historical progress; it does not see communism as a final state but only as a phase in a development which, in principle, has no end; but it has the courage to believe in a utopia.

In later years Marx saw that radiant far-off vision of a utopia in less vivid colours, but he never abandoned it. To the very end of his life he remained convinced that the positive abolition of private ownership of the means of production, the scientific nature of labour, the maximum substitution of machines for men would bring *the whole man* into being and enable him to unfold the full range of his potential abilities.

Marx (and Engels even more) at first believed that the whole man would be formed within the sphere of socially necessary, useful production by mastering machines and constantly changing the nature of his activity. But Marx later abandoned this notion. As early as in 1857–8, in the draft entitled *Grundrisse der Kritik der politischen Ökonomie* (*Foundations of the Critique of Political Economy*), he laid stress on the 'artistic scientific education of individuals as a result of time becoming free for everyone', but thought it possible that the 'immediate material process of production' might be divested of its form as 'necessity'.[23]

In his last work, the third volume of *Capital*, he revised this view.

The actual wealth of society, and the possibility of constantly expanding its reproduction process, therefore, do not depend upon the duration of surplus-labour, but upon its productivity and the more or less copious conditions of production under which it is performed. In fact, the realm of freedom actually begins only where labour which is determined by necessity and mundane considerations ceases; thus in the very nature of things it lies beyond the sphere of actual material production. Just as the savage must wrestle with Nature to satisfy his wants, to maintain and reproduce life, so must civilized man, and he must do so in all social formations and under all possible modes of production. With his development this realm of physical necessity expands as a result of his wants; but, at the same time, the forces of production which satisfy these wants also increase. Freedom in this field can only consist in socialized man, the associated producers, rationally regulating their interchange with Nature, bringing it under their common control, instead of being ruled by it as the blind forces of Nature; and achieving this with the least expenditure of energy and under conditions most favourable to, and worthy of, their human nature. But it nonetheless remains a realm of necessity. Beyond it begins that development of human energy which is an end in itself, the true realm of freedom, which, however, can blossom forth only with this realm of necessity as its basis. The shortening of the working-day is its basic prerequisite.[24]

The 'realm of freedom' beyond the narrow sphere of material production as the true realm of man, of man's flowering in the midst of science and art, love and serenity, community and personal freedom – this greatest of all utopias is outlined in the work of the young Marx and remains preserved in the works of his maturity and old age. For Marx, the quintessence of positive humanism was not 'abstract', monotonous labour which reduces man to a fragment of himself, but *creative* work, the development of the human potential which is its own goal.

2

CREATIVE LABOUR

For Marx, the outstanding achievement of Hegel's philosophy was above all 'that Hegel grasps the self-creation of man as a process . . . that he, therefore, grasps the nature of *labour*, and conceives objective man (true, because real man) as the result of his *own labour*'.[25]

'In short, Hegel conceives labour as man's *act of self-creation* (though in abstract terms) . . . as the demonstration of his alien being.'[26]

The animal is one with its life activity. It does not distinguish the aim itself. It is *its activity*. But man makes his life activity itself an object of his will and consciousness. He has a conscious life activity . . .

The practical construction of an *objective world*, the *manipulation* of inorganic nature, is the confirmation of man as a conscious species-being, i.e. a being who treats the species as his own being or himself as a species-being. Of course, animals also produce. They construct nests, dwellings, as in the case of bees, beavers, ants, etc. But they only produce what is strictly necessary for themselves or their young. They produce only in a single direction, while man produces universally. They produce only under the compulsion of direct physical need, while man produces when he is free from physical need and only truly produces in freedom from such need. Animals produce only themselves, while man reproduces the whole of nature. The products of animal production belong directly to their physical bodies, while man is free in face of his product . . .

It is just in his work upon the objective world that man really proves himself as a *species-being*. This production is his active species-life. By means of it nature appears as *his* work and his reality. The object of labour is, therefore, the *objectification of man's species-life;* for he no longer reproduces himself merely intellectually, as in consciousness, but actively and in a real sense, and he sees his own reflection in a world which he has constructed.[27]

Man as the creator of himself, as the product, capable of development and change, of his own labour, as a living being objectifying himself in his work and confronting himself in the reality he has created: that is the central theme of the philosophy Marx found already existing in rough outline when he grew up. He was to enrich it by a number of essential insights and to draw the consequences it implied. The striking thing about the *Economic and Political Manuscripts* – which, after all, were only a draft – is the manner in which the philosophical principle of labour is interlinked with the historical manifestations of labour. The fact that man 'only truly produces in freedom from physical need' is the anticipation of a state not yet achieved, or only sporadically achieved in history. But to perceive this creative nature of labour at its very origin was to discover the inexhaustible possibilities hidden in man as a working being.

This living being had emerged from nature in the darkness of time, representing nature and anti-nature at the same time, different from all other species by *conscious activity*. Marx was fully aware that many conditions must have combined to make this emergence possible, but he refused to become involved in biological or any other speculations based on fantasy rather than on science. What mattered to him was the new *quality* regardless of the processes which had created it: the essence of the new species: labour.

The species-nature of animals is an eternal repetition, that of man is transformation, development, change. An animal is the past incarnate in the present: man is not only past and present, but also the future. An animal accepts what nature offers; man forces nature to give him more. He lays hands on nature, enters into conflict with it, alienates himself from it and takes possession of what has become alien by making it serve his purpose – by *working* it.

Man *works himself out* of nature, forming his man-nature by his hands, his consciousness and his imagination in community with other men.

What, then, is labour – apparently so easy to define, but in reality open to so many definitions and in its effects so infinite?

Labour is, in the first place, a process in which both man and Nature participate, and in which man of his own accord starts, regulates, and controls the material reactions between himself and Nature. He opposes himself to Nature as one of her own forces, setting in motion arms and legs, head and hands, the natural forces of his body, in order to appropriate Nature's productions in a form adapted to his own wants. By thus acting on the external world and changing it, he at the same time changes his own nature. He develops his slumbering powers and compels them to act in obedience to his sway. We are not now dealing with those primitive instinctive forms of labour that remind us of the mere animal. An immeasurable interval of time separates the state of things in which a man brings his labour-power to market for sale as a commodity, from that state in which human labour was still in its first instinctive stage. We presuppose labour in a form that stamps it as exclusively human. A spider conducts operations that resemble those of a weaver, and a bee puts to shame many an architect in the construction of her cells. But what distinguishes the worst architect from the best of bees is this, that the architect raises his structure in imagination before he erects it in reality. At the end of every labour-process, we get a result that already existed in the imagination of the labourer at its commencement.[28]

In order to determine the nature of labour Marx presupposes it in an already developed form and takes account of the fact that it has a long history. Labour begins with the utilization of an 'occasional tool' found in nature and proceeds to the discovery that such tools can be reproduced and given a more efficient form. In other words, the means to achieve a purpose precedes the worker's sense of purpose, the ideal result anticipated in his imagination. Marx hints that labour must not be merely effort, not only a curse upon mankind condemned to labour by the sweat of its brow, but that it must carry the worker along as the 'play' of his own physical and spiritual forces, and thus unite the performance principle with the pleasure principle. In a polemic against Adam Smith, Marx opposed the *creative* principle inherent in labour to the 'historical forms of labour as slave, *corvée* or wage labour'. In these historical forms labour is *external compulsion* and has lost its purpose 'as self-realization, objectification of the subject, hence as the real freedom which its action constitutes'.[29]

The instinctive form of early labour was transcended by *instruments of labour*.

The use and fabrication of instruments of labour, although existing in the germ among certain species of animals, is specifically characteristic of the human labour-process, and Franklin therefore defines man as a tool-making animal. Relics of bygone instruments of labour possess the same importance for the investigation of extinct economic forms of society, as do fossil bones for the determination of extinct species of animals. It is not the articles made, but how they are made, and by what instruments, that enables us to distinguish different economic epochs. Instruments of labour not only supply a standard of the degree of development to which human labour has attained, but they are also indicators of the social conditions under which that labour is carried on . . .

In the labour-process, therefore, man's activity, with the help of the instruments of labour, effects an alteration, designed from the commencement, in the material worked upon. The process disappears in the product; the latter is a use-value, Nature's material adapted by a change of form to the wants of man. Labour has incorporated itself with its subject: the former is materialized, the latter transformed. That which in the labourer appeared as movement, now appears in the product as a fixed quality without motion.[30]

The interaction established by labour between man and natural substance manifests itself in the dual nature of labour as production and consumption:

Labour uses up its material factors, its subject and its instruments, consumes them, and is therefore a process of consumption. Such productive consumption is distinguished from individual consumption by this, that the latter uses up products, as means of subsistence for the living individual; the former, as means whereby alone, labour, the labour-power of the living individual, is enabled to act.[31]

But it is not only a question of labour consuming the natural substance: the natural substance also consumes the energy of the worker. When labour is creative, this energy is returned to the worker, not only as the work product – as humanized natural substance – but also as confirmation of his individuality and his latent potential.

The labour-process, resolved as above into its simple elementary factors, is human action with a view to the production of use-values, appropriation of natural substances to human requirements; it is the necessary condition for effecting exchange of matter between man and Nature; it is the everlasting Nature-imposed condition of human existence, and therefore is independent of every social phase of that existence, or rather, is common to every such phase.[32]

Before we turn to the historical forms of labour determined by the development of instruments of labour, by the increasing division of labour, by production of commodities for the market, by *having* and *ruling*, let us emphasize once more how much importance Marx always attached to the *principle of labour as man's species-nature*. To see labour as the anticipation of the work product is to see man as a being that projects, plans and constructs the future. The first tool contains within it all the potential future ones. The first recognition of the fact that the world can be changed by conscious activity contains all future, as yet unknown, but inevitable change. A living being which has once begun to make nature his own through the work of his hands, his intellect and his imagination, will never stop. Every achievement opens the door to unconquered territory.

But when labour is destructive, not creative, when it is undertaken under coercion and not as the free play of forces, when it means the withering, not the flowering, of man's physical and intellectual potential, then labour is a denial of its own principle and therefore of the principle of man.

3

DIVISION OF
LABOUR AND ALIENATION

In principle, labour is conceived as a *whole*, as man's species-nature, the collective creative activity of mankind. But if its possibilities are to be properly exploited and the full potential latent in mankind is to be activated, labour must become a *multiple* activity divided into many separate ones; for no individual and no community limited in place and time is capable of doing what mankind as a whole is called upon to do. In order, then, to become all-embracing, labour evolved a multitude of one-sided activities; in order to expand production, it was necessary to narrow down individual work processes, and in order to make possible a state of universal wealth – a plenitude of material and spiritual goods – the *enrichment of the few* and *poverty for the majority* were unavoidable for thousands of years.

The division of labour not only destroyed unity: by introducing inequality among the various occupations it created and reinforced social inequality. Labour was not, and still is not, divided up into equal parts, but is divided for the profit of the stronger and the disadvantage of the weaker.

Marx distinguishes between the *social* division of labour and the division of labour *in manufacture*, that is to say within society and within each work process. These two categories overlap and interlink continually.

If we keep labour alone in view, we may designate the separation of social production into its main division or *genera* – viz., agriculture, industries, etc. – as division of labour in general, and the splitting up of these families into species and sub-species, as division of labour in particular, and the division of labour within the workshop as division of labour in singular or in detail.[33]

The division of social production into its broad categories leads to the creation of private property and splits society up into haves and have-nots, rulers and ruled, exploiters and exploited.

Division of labour in a society, and the corresponding tying down of individuals to a particular calling, develops itself, just as does the division of labour in manufacture, from opposite starting points. Within a family and after further development within a tribe,* there springs up naturally a division of labour, caused by differences of sex and age, a division that is consequently based on a purely physiological foundation, which division enlarges its materials by the expansion of the community by the increase of population, and more especially, by the conflicts between different tribes, and the subjugation of one tribe by another.[34]

Marx drew attention repeatedly to the importance of conquest – territorial occupation – for social division of labour and the emergence of private property. We quote one such passage.

War is among the original labours of each of these primitive communities, both for the maintenance of property and for its acquisition. . . . If man is conquered along with land as being its organic accessory, he is conquered as one of the conditions of production, and this gives rise to slavery and serfdom, which soon falsify and change the original form of any community and become the basis for a new form.[35]

On the other hand . . . the exchange of products springs up at

* In the *Grundrisse*, which represent his preliminary work on *Capital*, Marx assumed the tribe – rather than the family – to be the original social unit. Subsequent scientific discoveries have confirmed this assumption.

the points where different families, tribes, communities, come in contact; for, in the beginning of civilization, it is not private individuals but families, tribes, etc., that meet on an independent footing. Different communities find different means of production and different means of subsistence in their natural environment. Hence, their modes of production and of living, and their products, are different. It is this spontaneously developed difference which, when different communities come in contact, calls forth the mutual exchange of products, and the consequent gradual conversion of those products into commodities. . . . The so-called division of labour arises from the exchange between spheres of production, that are originally distinct and independent of one another.[36]

Increasing population and production, power and commerce are, therefore, the necessary pre-conditions for the division of labour.

The greatest division of material and mental labour is the separation of town and country. The antagonism between town and country begins with the transition from barbarism to civilization, from tribe to State, from locality to nation, and runs through the whole history of civilization to the present day. . . . The existence of the town implies, at the same time, the necessity of administration, police, taxes, etc., in short, of the municipality, and thus of politics in general. Here first became manifest the division of the population into two great classes, which is directly based on the division of labour and on the instruments of production. The town already is in actual fact the concentration of the population, of the instruments of production, of capital, of pleasures, of needs, while the country demonstrates just the opposite fact, their isolation and separation. The antagonism of town and country can only exist as a result of private property. It is the most crass expression of the subjection of the individual under the division of labour, under a definite activity forced upon him – a subjection which makes one man into a restricted town-animal, the other into a restricted country-animal, and daily creates anew the conflict between their interests.[37]

The division of labour, both socially and in manufacture, entails not only the development and objectification of the potential gifts latent in the human race, but also 'a certain mental and physical crippling'.[38]

The craftsman was still at home with himself, producing something rounded and complete, for all its limitations.

In the towns, the division of labour between the individual guilds was as yet quite natural, and, in the guilds themselves, not at all developed between the individual workers. Every workman had to be versed in a whole round of tasks, had to be able to make everything that was to be made with his tools. The limited commerce and the scanty communication between the individual towns, the lack of population and the narrow needs did not allow of a higher division of labour, and therefore every man who wished to become a master had to be proficient in the whole of his craft. Thus there is found with medieval craftsmen an interest in their special work and a proficiency in it, which was capable of rising to a narrow artistic sense. For this very reason, however, every medieval craftsman was completely absorbed in his work, to which he had a contented, slavish relationship, and to which he was subjected to a far greater extent than the modern worker whose work is a matter of indifference to him.[39]

The personal relationship of the craftsman to his product first began to change with the manufacturing systems, in which division of labour began to predominate. But the later introduction of machinery led to a radical depersonalization of the worker.

In the first place, in the form of machinery, the implements of labour become automatic, things moving and working independent of the workman. They are thenceforth an industrial *perpetuum mobile* that would go on producing forever, it did not meet with certain natural obstructions in the weak bodies and the strong wills of its human attendants.[40]

Along with the tool, the skill of the workman in handing it

passes over to the machine. The capabilities of the tool are emancipated from the restraints that are inseparable from human labour-power. Thereby the technical foundation on which is based the division of labour in Manufacture, is swept away. Hence, in the place of the hierarchy of specialized workmen that characterizes manufacture, there steps, in the automatic factory, a tendency to equalize and reduce to one and the same level every kind of work that has to be done by the minders of the machines, in the place of the artificially produced differentiations of the detail workmen, step the natural differences of age and sex.[41]

In handicrafts and manufacture, the workman makes use of a tool, in the factory, the machine makes use of him. There the movements of the instrument of labour proceed from him, here it is the movements of the machine that he must follow. In manufacture the workmen are parts of a living mechanism. In the factory we have a lifeless mechanism independent of the workman, who becomes its mere living appendage . . .

At the same time that factory work exhausts the nervous system to the uttermost, it does away with the many-sided play of the muscles, and confiscates every atom of freedom, both in bodily and intellectual activity. The lightening of the labour, even, becomes a sort of torture, since the machine does not free the labourer from work, but deprives the work of all interest . . . The special skill of each individual insignificant factory operative vanishes as an infinitesimal quantity before the science, the gigantic physical forces, and the mass of labour that are embodied in the factory mechanism and, together with that mechanism, constitute the power of the 'master' . . .

The technical subordination of the workman to the uniform motion of the instruments of labour, and the peculiar composition of the body of workpeople, consisting as it does of individuals of both sexes and of all ages, give rise to a barrack discipline, which is elaborated into a complete system in the factory, and which fully develops the beforementioned labour of overlooking, thereby dividing the workpeople into operatives and overlookers, into private soldiers and sergeants of an industrial army.[42]

Thus labour in its historical development becomes the negation of its own principle, that of creative activity through which man makes himself: instead, man makes himself into an accessory of the machine, a partial function in the mechanism of the instruments of labour which dominate him. But Marx the dialectician sees not only the negation but also, at the same time, the counter-tendency growing with it and because of it.

Modern Industry never looks upon and treats the existing form of a process as final. The technical basis of that industry is therefore revolutionary, while all earlier modes of production were essentially conservative. By means of machinery, chemical processes and other methods, it is continually causing changes not only in the technical basis of production, but also in the functions of the labourers, and in the social combinations of the labour-process. At the same time, it thereby also revolutionizes the division of labour within the society, and incessantly launches masses of capital and of workpeople from one branch of production to another. But if Modern Industry, by its very nature, therefore necessitates variation of labour, fluency of function, universal mobility of the labourer, on the other hand, in its capitalistic form, it reproduces the old division of labour with its ossified particularizations. . . . This is the negative side. But if, on the one hand, variation of work at present imposes itself after the manner of an overpowering natural law, and with the blindly destructive action of a natural law that meets with resistance at all points, Modern Industry, on the other hand, through its catastrophes imposes the necessity of recognizing, as a fundamental law of production, variation of work, consequently fitness of the labourer for varied work, consequently the greatest possible development of his varied aptitudes. It becomes a question of life and death for society to adapt the mode or production to the normal functioning of this law. Modern Industry, indeed, compels society, under penalty of death, to replace the detail-worker of today, crippled by lifelong repetition of one and the same trivial operation, by the fully developed individual, fit for a variety of labours, ready to face any change of production, and to whom the different social functions he performs, are but so many modes of giving free scope to his own natural and acquiring powers.[43]

Marx explained the pre-conditions which were inevitably bound to lead to the division of labour; and, equally inevitably, the division of labour was bound to lead to the division of common property and the transition to *private ownership*.

The division of labour implies from the outset the division of the *conditions of labour*, of tools and materials, and thus the splitting up of accumulated capital among different owners, and thus also the division between capital and labour, and the different forms of property itself. The more the division of labour develops and accumulation grows, the sharper are the forms that this process of differentiation assumes. Labour itself can only exist on the premise of this fragmentation.

Thus two facts are here revealed. First, the productive forces appear as a world for themselves, quite independent of and divorced from the individuals, alongside the individuals: the reason for this is that the individuals, whose forces they are, exist split up and in opposition to one another, whilst on the other hand these forces are only real forces in the intercourse and association of these individuals. Thus, on the one hand, we have a totality of productive forces, which have, as it were, taken on a material form and are for the individuals no longer the forces of the individuals but of private property, and hence of the individuals only in so far as they are owners of private property themselves. . . . On the other hand, standing over against these productive forces, we have the majority of the individuals from whom these forces have been wrested away, and who, robbed thus of all real life-content, have become abstract individuals, but who are, however, only by this fact put into a position to enter into relation with one another *as individuals*.

The only connexion which still links them with the productive forces and with their own existence – labour – has lost all semblance of self-activity and only sustains their life by stunting it. While in the earlier periods self-activity and the production of material life were separated, in that they devolved on different persons, and while, on account of the narrowness of the individuals themselves, the production of material life was considered as a subordinate mode of self-activity, they now diverge to such an extent that finally material life appears as the end, and what produces this material life, labour (which is not the only possible but, as we see, negative form of self-activity), as the means.[44]

This is a thought that recurs again and again in Marx: material life is the *basis*, but not the *purpose*, of human existence. The fact that labour appears only as a means of sustaining life, no longer as creative activity by which man makes and moulds himself, is for Marx a contradiction of the nature of man: when he says, therefore, that economic conditions are more powerful than the individual, that is not, for him, an eternal law but a stage of historical development, the transcending of which is the great task of humanity. The economy must not dominate man: it must be brought under the control of a humanity made up of associated individuals.

The division of labour offers the example

of how, as long as man remains in natural society, that is as long as a cleavage exists between the particular and the common interest, as long therefore as activity is not voluntarily, but naturally, divided, man's own deed becomes an alien power opposed to him, which enslaves him instead of being controlled by him. . . . This crystallization of social activity, this consolidation of what we ourselves produce into an objective power above us, growing out of our control, thwarting our expectations, bringing to naught our calculations, is one of the chief factors in historical development up till now. And out of this very contradiction between the interest of the individual and that of the community the latter takes an independent form as the *State*, divorced from the real interest of individual and community . . .

The social power, i.e. the multiplied productive force, which arises through the co-operation of different individuals as it is determined within the division of labour, appears to these individuals, since their co-operation is not voluntary but natural, not as their own united power but as an alien force existing outside them, of the origin and end of which they are ignorant, which they thus cannot control, which on the contrary passes through a peculiar series of phases and stages independent of the will and the action of man, nay even being the prime governor of these. This 'estrangement' (to use a term which will be comprehensible to the philosophers) can, of course, only be abolished given two *practical* premises . . .

Marx thought that these two practical premises were, first, that the contradiction between the great mass of non-property-owning humanity and the 'existing world of wealth and culture' had to become 'intolerable', and, secondly, that productive forces had to develop universally and not only in a few countries, 'for the reason that without this, only *want* is made general, and with want the struggle for necessities would necessarily be reproduced'.[45]

Thus it is the division of labour with all its consequences – private ownership of the means of production and the products of labour, domination of the product over the producer, the totality of productive forces and institutions, State, church, justice, etc., confronting the individual as alien forces, which produce the state Marx called *alienation*. Men, with the exception of a tiny minority engaged in creative activity, cannot recognize themselves in their own works; social production exists as a 'fatality exterior to themselves',[46] creation overshadows the creator, and this 'second' nature which man has wrested from original, elementary nature appears even more powerful, even less controllable than the first with its famines, earthquakes and eruptions. The material relationship has grown beyond all individual things and has become an autonomous power.

In a world of advanced division of labour, of private ownership of the materials, instruments and products of labour, of institutions and ideologies, of *having* and *ruling*, alienation is generalized: not only the worker who sells his labour but also the employer who appropriates the product of another man's work and the merchant who takes the commodity to market, the 'haves' and the 'have-nots', the rulers and the ruled, are, in such a world, alienated from their work, from others and from themselves. In many ways it is a world upside down, where objects, appropriated by man, acquire the crazy power of owning men.

Already in feudal land-ownership the ownership of the earth appears as an alien power ruling over men. The serf is the product of the land. In the same way the heir, the first-born son, belongs to the land. It inherits him.[47]

The worker's alienation is the most extreme form because it is the very nature of his activity; for the non-worker, the master, the owner, the idler, alienation is not an activity but a condition.

DIFFERENTIAL ALIENATION

It should be noted first that everything which appears to the worker as an *activity of alienation*, appears to the non-worker as a *condition of alienation*.[48]

When, at an earlier stage in history, two tribes met at a prearranged place and exchanged gifts, that was not an act of alienation but of encounter, of human approach. As soon as the object that had once been a gift became a commodity, trust gave way to mistrust and generous exchange to calculation. What now passed from hand to hand was no longer the *expression* of a group of people but its *alienation* in the work product, and one side no longer admired the objective and special quality in the object offered by the other but was interested only in its general quality, its *exchange value* weighed against the exchange value of something else.

Originally, exchange 'both of human activity within production itself and of *human products* against one another . . . = *species activity* and *species spirit*, whose real, conscious and true existence is *social* activity and *social* enjoyment.'[49] When this original exchange becomes commodity exchange, and when common property becomes private property, the real community of men is transformed into a caricature of itself. Commodity exchange mediates social intercourse; the *bond of essential nature* that links one man to another 'appears as an inessential bond'; 'instead, man's separation from other men appears as his true existence'; 'his power over the object appears as the power of the object over him, the lord of creation appears as the slave of his creation'.[50]

The political economy of bourgeois society

comprehends the community of men, or their active *human nature*, their completion of one another making up their species life, their truly human life, under the form of exchange and commerce. . . . 'Society', says Adam Smith, 'is a trading society. Each of its members is a merchant.'[51]

In commodity exchange, in trade, objects gain power over men; the object offered to another no longer represents the community that offers it; the trader represents the object he is offering for sale. The face of man disappears behind the merchant's social character mask. The community of *competition*, the trading society, manifests itself as estrangement – as *alienation*.

Just as for the man who takes his commodities to market the commodity becomes the *subject* and he himself only *a function*, individuals become functionaries – officials – in the hierarchy of social institutions. Other men do not see them as fellow-men having equal rights, but as superiors or subordinates, as holders of a rank, as a small or large unit of power. Every functionary is alienated from every other functionary and all of them are alienated from the simple citizen. Likewise the owner and the man who sells his labour are alienated from one another: and, while in small-scale agriculture and in artisan trade such alienation still retains certain features (which may often be hypocritical) of familiarity and trust, in large-scale industry it is undisguised. In other words, while alienation is the universal characteristic of production based on exchange values and the increasing division of labour which such production entails, it assumes its most extreme form in the case of the wage labourer, the man who sells his labour as a commodity – in his relationship to his work product, the work process, and himself.

In labour for gain the following are inherent: (1) the alienation of work from the working subject, and its arbitrary nature; (2) the arbitrary nature and alienation of the work from its object; (3) the determining of the worker by social wants which, however, are alien to him and a constraint upon him, to which he submits only out of selfish want, out of need, and which for him mean only a source of satisfaction of his needs, just as he exists for society only as a slave of *its* needs; (4) the fact that to the worker the maintenance of his individual existence appears as the purpose of his activity, and his real activity only as a means; that he activates his life in order to gain the means of maintaining his life (means of subsistence).

Hence, the greater and more formed the power of society appears within the private property relation, the more selfish, unsocial, alienated from his own nature does man become.[52]

In an age when this alienation of man from his nature, this antisocial egoism, this reduction of labour to empty wage-earning, to a 'job', has come to be accepted without question, it is doubly important to remind ourselves of Marx's protest against alienation, selfishness, and the deformation of labour, against brutal materialism raised to the status of a principle.

Although workers in the most advanced industrial societies are no longer the wretched slaves they were in Marx's time, we can still recognize the essential truth of hard, concrete formulations such as this:

We have now considered the act of alienation of practical human activity, labour, from two aspects: (1) the relationship of the worker to the *product of labour* as an alien object which dominates him. This relationship is at the same time the relationship to the sensuous external world, to natural objects, as an alien and hostile world; (2) the relationship of the worker to the *act of production* within *labour*. This is the relationship of the worker to his own activity as something alien and not belonging to him, activity as suffering (passivity), strength as powerlessness, creation as emasculation, the *personal* physical and mental energy of the worker, his personal life (for what is life but activity?), as an activity which is directed against himself, independent of him and not belonging to him. This is *self-alienation* as against the above-mentioned alienation of the thing.[53]

Because Marx saw the 'species-nature of man' in creative activity, in man's conscious transformation of the outside world and consequently in his all-round *self-realization*, the loss of the creative quality of labour meant to him man's alienation from his species-nature and therefore from himself.

If man's relationship to himself is simply a relationship to a living creature that is obliged to work in order to maintain itself – if his activity is not the universal free play of forces but simply *earning* – if his labour has become a commodity and he merely a thing unto himself, then he ceases, as an individual, to represent mankind.

. . . A direct consequence of the alienation of man from the product of his labour, from his life activity and from his species-life, is that *man* is *alienated* from other *men*. When man confronts himself he also confronts other *men*. What is true of man's relationship to his work, to the product of his work and to himself, is also true of his relationship to other men, to their labour and to the objects of their labour.

In general, the statement that man is alienated from his species-life means that each man is alienated from others, and that each of the others is likewise alienated from human life.

Human alienation, and above all the relation of man to himself, is first realized and expressed in the relationship between each man and other men. Thus in the relationship of alienated labour every man regards other men according to the standards and relationships in which he finds himself placed as a worker.[54]

In a *society of alienation* the relationship of a man with other men is not that of a human being to his fellow human beings but that of a servant to his master, of an exploited man to his exploiter, of a subordinate to his commander, a petitioner to a man of privilege, and so forth, to include all the many ranks and degrees of social status allotted to everyone.

The division of labour within the work process reduces the worker to a component of a massive piece of machinery, to some detailed function which renders the work contentless and its performer a fragment of a man: what he produces does not matter to him: the product of his work is not objectification of his own self but something removed from his grasp.

The social division of labour, which makes one man the owner of materials, instruments of labour and products and another man a dispossessed creature who takes his labour to market and merely performs the act of production without having any share in determining it, precludes any *productive community* in which every talent would have an equal chance and where production would be determined, not by profit, but by the common material and intellectual interest in the all-round development of man.

The contradiction between the actual socialization of production and the fragmentation of property among a multitude of private interests denies the producers any control over the movement of their products, subjects them to the autonomous power of the products, and distorts human society into a society ruled by things, where man's works oppose him as something alien to him, an alien world of historical 'natural laws', mysterious forces of destiny, powerful institutions, gigantic fetishes.

Marx believed that this 'confusion and transposition' of man's nature is historically conditioned and can for that reason be overcome. Certainly the objective conditions of labour, the technical and administrative machinery, take on 'an ever more colossal independence' *vis-à-vis* living labour itself, and social wealth opposes labour 'in increasingly tremendous proportion as an alien and dominant force'. But this 'process of transposition' is

merely *historical* necessity, merely a necessity for the development of the productive forces from a certain historical starting point or basis, but by no means an *absolute* necessity of production; rather, a disappearing one, and the [immanent] result and goal of this process is to abolish this basis itself, as well as this form of the process.[55]

The problem of alienation was for Marx a central problem and not, as is frequently asserted nowadays, a romantic humanist notion of the young Marx, 'Marx in his anti-Marxist and pre-Marxist phase'. Certainly there was a young Marx and an older one, but there was no such thing as an 'anti-Marxist' and a 'Marxist' Marx. The *Grundrisse der Kritik der politischen Ökonomie* were written in 1857–8, when Marx was forty years old: the concept of alienation is as alive in this work as in any previous one. But it is true that the hope that the 'objective moments of production can be divested of alienation' is supplanted in the last volume of *Capital* – Marx's last work – by the thought that man can only become a *whole man*, that is to say a man no longer alienated from himself and his fellow-men, when he has advanced beyond the sphere of production for the sake of necessity.

4

THE FETISH CHARACTER
OF THE COMMODITY

The declaration of 'inalienable' human rights pre-supposes a world in which everything has been alienated: let human rights, at least, be kept outside the dirty game. Everything has become a commodity: side by side with the meat market there is the art market, side by side with the car market is the book market, the labour market, the sex market, markets for information, secret services and, of course, public opinion. Above all it is man who becomes a commodity:

> Production does not only produce man as a *commodity*, the *human commodity*, man in the form of a *commodity*; in conformity with this situation it produces him as a *mentally* and *physically* dehumanized being . . .[56]
> The worker becomes an ever cheaper commodity the more goods he creates. The *devaluation* of the human world increases in direct relation with the increase in value of the world of things.[57]

The young Marx was wrong when he assumed that the worker must become 'cheaper', i.e. more wretched, with the growth of production. But the dictum that the devaluation of the human world increases with the increase in value of the world of things remains valid. We have become so accustomed to living in a world of commodities, where nature is perhaps only a poster for a holiday resort and man only an advertisement for a new product, we exist in such a turmoil of alienated objects offered cheaply for sale, that we hardly ask ourselves any longer what it is that magically transforms objects of necessity (or fashion) into commodities and what is the true nature of the witches' sabbath, ablaze with neon moons and synthetic constellations, that has become our day-to-day reality.

What, then, is a commodity?

A commodity is in the first place an object outside us, a thing that by its properties satisfies human wants of some sort or another. The nature of such wants, whether, for instance, they spring from the stomach or from fancy, makes no difference. Neither are we here concerned to know how the object satisfies these wants, whether directly as means of subsistence or indirectly as means of production . . .

The utility of a thing makes it a use-value. . . . This property of a commodity is independent of the amount of labour required to appropriate its useful qualities. . . . Use-values become a reality only by use or consumption: they also constitute the substance of all wealth, whatever may be the social form of that wealth. In the form of society we are about to consider, they are, in addition, the material depositories of exchange value.[58]

Between the use-values of objects – bread or drugs, dwelling-houses or weapons – nothing is comparable; the only thing they have in common is that they are used for consumption, production or destruction. But as exchange values – as commodities – objects are reduced to something comparable, measurable, common to them all.

This common 'something' cannot be either a geological, a chemical or any other natural property of commodities. Such properties claim our attention only in so far as they affect the utility of those commodities, make them use-values. But the exchange of commodities is evidently an act characterized by a total abstraction from use-value . . .

As use-values, commodities are, above all, of different

qualities, but as exchange-values they are merely different quantities, and consequently do not contain an atom of use-value.

If then we leave out of consideration the use-value of commodities, they have only one common property left, that of being products of labour. But even the product of labour has undergone a change in our hands . . .

When a table, a house or a bale of cotton are mutually exchanged in a certain, by no means arbitrary, ratio, all their sensuous properties are wiped out by this act (although it has previously been ascertained that they possess these sensuous properties in the desired quantity, i.e. that the apple is not rotten and the table not badly made). In the act of exchange all these useful characteristics of the work product have not disappeared, and neither have the concrete forms of the labour required for their production: rather, they are all reduced to one and the same sort of labour, human labour in the abstract.

Let us now consider the residue of each of these products: it consists of the same unsubstantial reality in each, a mere congelation of homogeneous human labour, of labour-power expended without regard to the mode of its expenditure. All that these things now tell us is, that human power has been expended in their production, that human labour is embodied in them. When looked at as crystals of this social substance, common to them all, they are – Values.[59] *

A commodity appears, at first sight, a very trivial thing, and easily understood. Its analysis shows that it is, in reality, a very queer thing, abounding in metaphysical subtleties and theological niceties. . . . So far as it is a value in use, there is nothing mysterious about it. . . . The form of wood, for instance, is

* It would take up too much space to comment, even tentatively, on Marx's highly complex theory of exchange value, the objections raised to it and the attempts made to refute it. We are deliberately confining ourselves to the enigmatic fetish character of the commodity as one of the concrete manifestations of the general alienation which is the result and the pre-condition of a society based on commodity production.

altered by making a table out of it. Yet, for all that, the table continues to be that common, everyday thing, wood. But, so soon as it steps forth as a commodity, it is changed into something transcendent. It not only stands with its feet on the ground, but, in relation to all other commodities, it stands on its head, and evolves out of its wooden brain grotesque ideas, far more wonderful than 'table-turning' ever was.[60]

A motor-car as use-value has nothing enigmatic about it but as a commodity it is so capricious and unaccountable that not only the buyer but also, and especially, the producer is confronted with new riddles at every step. Only yesterday the demand was all for great big pompous limousines as status symbols: today, all of a sudden, they have become unsaleable; the plain-looking, solid family car is all the rage; then suddenly this too begins to falter, and firms which dominated the market are faced with collapse. Market analysis, psychology and publicity keep the commodity under some sort of control: then, quite unexpectedly, it begins to behave in a way 'far more wonderful than table-turning ever was'.

This wilfulness of the commodity is an expression of the contradiction between the *social* nature of production and the apparently 'independent' producer. This so-called independent producer is, whether he wants it or not, dependent on the social totality, on the price of raw materials and labour, on the average productivity of labour, on demand and supply, on the consumers' requirements and purchasing power. Thus the commodity becomes the objectification of the inner contradiction of 'private economy' in a world of all-embracing social production.

There is a definite social relation between men, that assumes, in their eyes, the fantastic form of a relation between things. In order, therefore, to find an analogy, we must have recourse to the mist-enveloped regions of the religious world. In that world the productions of the human brain appear as independent beings endowed with life, and entering into relations both with one another and the human race. So it is in the world of commodities with the products of men's hands. This I call the Fetishism which attaches itself to the products of labour, so soon as they are produced as commodities, and which is therefore inseparable from the production of commodities . . .

. . . articles of utility become commodities, only because they are products of the labour of private individuals or groups of individuals who carry on their work independently of each other. The sum total of the labour of all these private individuals forms the aggregate labour of society. Since the producers do not come into social contact with each other until they exchange their products, the specific social character of each producer's labour does not show itself except in the act of exchange. In other words, the labour of the individual asserts itself as a part of the labour of society, only by means of the relations which the act of exchange establishes directly between the products, and indirectly, through them, between the producers. To the latter, therefore, the relations connecting the labour of one individual with that of the rest appear, not as direct social relations between individuals at work, but as what they really are, material relations between persons and social relations between things.[61]

It is in the commodity that the doubling – or rather, trebling – of the world by human activity manifests itself. A commodity is an object of *nature*, made out of nature's elements. It is a product of *labour*, that is to say an object designed and formed by man to serve a specific purpose. And it is an object that lets in the 'super-sensory', the *social*, the structure of a society based on private property and the division of labour. In this threefold reality it hides the secret of a still deeper contradiction: it is the *single* thing that relates – without its owner's knowledge – to a whole, a private thing that socializes itself. Even when it appears most individual, it relates to general demand and general labour. It brings profit today and disaster tomorrow; its price rises and falls, its value is diminished because a more productive method of work has been introduced somewhere else; it is wooed when it has no rivals, rejected when it has too many, it can start a crisis or even a war, and its possessor seems to be obsessed by it.

The more all-embracing the total labour (and total demand) of human beings on the one hand and the more complex and manifold the division of labour on the other, the greater becomes the power of the densely woven, opaque relationships between things. The social character of labour prevails in the commodity form of the work products. Quite often it will defeat the plans of the private producer or owner, make nonsense of his calculations, sweep everything before it like a force of nature, correct by catastrophe the false relationship between the totality of labour and demand, on the one hand, and the arbitrariness of *having* on the other. The work product as commodity has overpowered its producer, and, by objectifying all relationships, has dehumanized them.

In simpler social structures, in the past, the relationships between people had not been rendered invisible by the relationships between things. In medieval Europe the dependence of the serf on the lord of the manor, of the vassal on the feudal lord, had not yet been transformed into apparent independence hemmed in on all sides by material relations.

Personal dependence here characterizes the social relations of production just as much as it does the other spheres of life organized on the basis of that production. But for the very reason that personal dependence forms the ground-work of society, there is no necessity for labour and its products to assume a fantastic form different from their reality. They take the shape, in the transactions of society, of services in kind and payments in kind. Here the particular and natural form of labour, and not, as in society based on production of commodities, its general abstract form is the immediate social form of labour. Compulsory labour is just as properly measured by time, as commodity-producing labour; but every serf knows that what he expends in the service of the lord is a definite quantity of his own personal labour-power. The tithe to be rendered to the priest is more matter of fact than his blessing. No matter, then, what we may think of the parts played by the different classes of people themselves in this society, the social relations between individuals in the performance of their labour, appear at all events as their own mutual personal relations, and are not disguised under the shape of social relations between the products of labour.[62]

Marx certainly felt no nostalgia for this state of affairs; he saw the *materialization of power*, despite all its negative features, as that social form, 'wherein a system of universal social metabolism, of universal relationships, many-sided needs and universal capacities first comes into being',[63] as the historical transition to a society of free individuals on the basis of their communal, social productivity. But he was anxious to render visible the human beings at work behind the material relations.

Commodities cannot go to market and make exchanges of their own account. We must, therefore, have recourse to their guardians, who are also their owners. . . . In order that these objects may enter into relation with each other as commodities, their guardians must place themselves in relation to one another, as persons whose will resides in those objects, and must behave in such a way that each does not appropriate the commodity of the other, and part with his own, except by means of an act done by mutual consent. . . . The persons exist for one another merely as representatives of, and, therefore, as owners of commodities. In the course of our investigation we shall find, in general, that the characters who appear on the economic stage are but the personifications of the economic relations that exist between them.[64]

The important thing is not the individual commodity owner who obeys the law of the commodity because otherwise it would refuse him the right of ownership; important are the economic conditions which, though they are more powerful than any individual, can only be changed, transformed, revolutionized by united individuals.

Today no one thinks it an ultra-radical notion to suggest that the commodity owner in the world of modern productive forces should not simply be the representative, the spokesman of *his* commodity: that it is necessary to introduce at least a minimum of co-ordination between labour and demand on the one hand and private interest on the other; that the market cannot be the only regulator, that the commodity cannot be allowed to cause havoc in the name of freedom. The idea of planning is taking root.

But the commodity as a form of alienation will only be abolished when wealth and poverty, extravagance and misery, the power of the few to dispose of the production of the many and the subjugation of the many to the silent or grandiloquent rule of the few, have ceased to confront one another and the world has become a totality: when shortage is no longer the dictator: when plenty has been achieved as the fruit of labour liberated and united by science, the communal spirit, and the co-determination of all.

Today we are still ruled by the commodity and its abstraction – money.

The power of things over men in a society based on commodity production is concentrated in the power of money: of gold.

> . . . damned earth,
> Thou common whore of mankind, that putt'st odds
> Among the rout of nations . . .
>
> O thou sweet king-killer, and dear divorce
> 'Twixt natural son and sire! thou bright defiler
> Of Hymen's purest bed! thou valiant Mars!

> Thou ever young, fresh, lov'd, and delicate wooer,
> Whose blush doth thaw the consecrated snow
> That lies on Dian's lap! thou visible god,
> That solder'st close impossibilities,
> And mak'st them kiss!

It was not a red revolutionary, but William Shakespeare who wrote those lines. Marx quoted them, adding:

Since money, as the existing and active concept of value, confounds and exchanges everything, it is the universal *confusion and transportation* of all things, the inverted world, the confusion and transposition of all natural and human qualities.[65]

Marx has an answer to this depersonalization, this alienation and dehumanization by money, which is the measure and the commodity of all commodities.

Let us assume *man* to be *man*, and his relation to the world to be a human one. Then love can only be exchanged for love, trust for trust, etc. If you wish to enjoy art you must be an artistically cultivated person; if you wish to influence other people you must be a person who really has a stimulating and encouraging effect upon others. Every one of your relations to man and to nature must be a *specific expression*, corresponding to the object of your will, of your *real individual* life. If you love without evoking love in return, i.e. if you are not able, by the *manifestation* of yourself as a loving person, to make yourself a *beloved* person, then your love is impotent and a misfortune.[66]

But where is the force that can 'assume man to be man' and transform a world of fetishes, of confusion and transposition of all values, into a human world?

5

CLASSES AND
THE CLASS STRUGGLE

> The history of all hitherto existing society is the
> history of class struggle.[67]

Marx was not the discoverer, still less the 'inventor' of classes
and of the class struggle. That such things exist was already
known to Livy, Machiavelli, Adam Smith, Sismondi, Thierry,
Guizot, Thiers, Carlyle and many other historians, economists
and sociologists. Only in the Germany and Austria of the Holy
Alliance, that hotch-potch of princely courts and cottages,
privileges and backwardness, guilds and censorship, state
occasions and states of emergency, were classes unknown or
ignored, and the class struggle was seen as the machination of
subversive foreigners.

Marx's contribution to the theory of classes and class struggle
consisted in the following:

1. The attempt to determine the characteristics of a class.
2. The analysis of the origin of classes.
3. The recognition that the interests of one class at any given
time coincide with the development of the productive forces
and their impulse towards new social structures, whilst other
classes defend the established and the traditional because these
correspond to their interests.
4. The conviction that the proletariat is the last of the classes
and that its liberation demands the abolition of all classes and
the classless, rulerless society.

The social division of labour has given rise to the formation of professional groups of all kinds and, after a lengthy development, of *classes*.

Smiths, potters, carpenters, tailors, cobblers, stonemasons, etc. – all of them artisans – were able to constitute themselves as a class under specific historical conditions, those of the medieval town. In modern society they no longer form a class; they are wage labourers, entrepreneurs or 'self-employed' workers employing no hired help.

Doctors, teachers, philosophers, writers, artists are all 'intellectuals', but the 'intelligentsia' is not a class.

Landowners, yeoman farmers, villeins, serfs, agricultural labourers are in a position of antagonism against town dwellers; yet they do not form a class. The class division cuts across them.

In the earlier epochs of history, we find almost everywhere a complicated arrangement of society into various orders, a manifold gradation of social rank. In ancient Rome we have patricians, knights, plebeians, slaves; in the Middle Ages, feudal lords, vassals, guild-masters, journeymen, apprentices, serfs; in almost all these classes, again, subordinate gradations.

The modern bourgeois society that has sprouted from the ruins of feudal society has not done away with class antagonisms. It has but established new classes, new conditions of oppression, new forms of struggle in place of the old ones.

Our epoch, the epoch of the bourgeoisie, possesses, however, this distinctive feature: it has simplified the class antagonisms. Society as a whole is more and more splitting up into two great hostile camps, into two great classes directly facing each other: Bourgeoisie and Proletariat.[68]

Later, Marx was to correct this over-simplification, taking greater account of the multiplicity of society and defining more clearly the special characteristics of the most important classes.

But in the first place let it be emphasized that classes are not rigid nor unchangeable, nor are they something given from the beginning of time, but products of historical development, whilst also being the motive forces of that development.

From the 'chartered burgesses' of the earliest towns developed 'the first elements of the bourgeoisie':

. . . Out of the many local corporations of burghers there arose only gradually the burgher *class*. The conditions of life of the individual burghers became, on account of their antagonism to the existing relationships and of the mode of labour determined by these, conditions which were common to them all and independent of each individual. The burghers had created the conditions in so far as they had torn themselves free from feudal ties, and were created by them in so far as they were determined by their antagonism to the feudal system which they found in existence. When the individual towns began to enter into associations, these common conditions developed into class conditions. The same conditions, the same antagonisms, the same interests necessarily called forth on the whole similar customs everywhere. The bourgeoisie itself, with its conditions, develops only gradually, splits according to the division of labour into various fractions and finally absorbs all earlier possessing classes (while it develops the majority of the earlier non-possessing, and a part of the earlier possessing, classes into a new class, the proletariat) in the measure to which all earlier property is transformed into industrial or commercial capital. The separate individuals form a class only in so far as they have to carry on a common battle against another class; otherwise they are on hostile terms with each other as competitors. On the other hand, the class in its turn achieves an independent existence over against the individuals, so that the latter find their conditions of existence predestined, and hence have their position in life and their personal development assigned to them by their class, become subsumed under it.[69]

The important points here are that classes develop out of

common special interests in order to wage a common battle against other common special interests which are antagonistic to theirs and which have been elevated to the status of 'general' interests; that this battle is necessary for the classes to be able to constitute themselves as such; that in the battle, diverse strata of the population are drawn in and absorbed into the class being constituted; that classes formed in this way are in a constant state of inner movement, splitting up into fractions, becoming reunited under new conditions; that class interests assume an independent character *vis-à-vis* separate individuals, and the antagonism is always being in practice destroyed and created; in short, that classes are not immutable, monolithic formations but are forever changing, developing, differentiating themselves, whilst at the same time the common element always comes to the fore and integrates the individual within the class.

Each step in the development of the bourgeoisie was accompanied by a corresponding political advance of that class. An oppressed class under the sway of the feudal nobility, an armed and self-governing association in the medieval commune ('Commune' was the name taken, in France, by the nascent towns even before they had conquered from their feudal lords and masters local self-government and political rights as the 'Third Estate'); here independent urban republic (as in Italy and Germany), there taxable 'third estate' of the monarchy (as in France), afterwards, in the period of manufacture proper, serving either the semi-feudal or the absolute monarchy as a counterpose against the nobility, and, in fact, cornerstone of the great monarchies in general, the bourgeoisie has at last, since the establishment of Modern Industry and of the world market, conquered for itself, in the modern representative State, exclusive political sway.[70]

Not only the bourgeoisie but the proletariat, too, has gone through a lengthy history of development, a history which is as yet by no means concluded. 'The bourgeoisie begins with a proletariat which is itself a relic of the proletariat of feudal times.'[71]

Runaway serfs, dispossessed peasants, poverty-stricken artisans and journeymen, beggars, tramps, 'outsiders' first deprived of work and then herded together in workhouses – it was the poor, to put it quite simply, who formed the original proletariat.

In the last third of the fifteenth, and the first decade of the sixteenth century . . . a mass of free proletarians was hurled on the labour-market by the breaking up of the bands of feudal retainers, who, as Sir James Steuart well says, 'everywhere uselessly filled house and castle' . . . The rapid rise of the Flemish wool manufacturers, and the corresponding rise in the price of wool in England, gave the direct impulse to these evictions. The old nobility had been devoured by the great feudal wars. The new nobility was the child of its time, for which money was the power of all powers. Transformation of arable land into sheep-walks was, therefore, its cry. . . . The dwellings of the peasants and the cottages of the labourers were razed to the ground or doomed to decay . . .

The process of forcible expropriation of the people received in the sixteenth century a new and frightful impulse from the Reformation, and from the consequent colossal spoliation of the church property. The Catholic church was, at the time of the Reformation, feudal proprietor of a great part of the English land. The suppression of the monasteries, etc., hurled their inmates into the proletariat . . .

Even in the last decade of the seventeenth century the yeomanry, the class of independent peasants, were more numerous than the class of farmers. They had formed the backbone of Cromwell's strength. . . . About 1750 the yeomanry had disappeared, and so had, in the last decade of the eighteenth century, the last trace of the common land of the agricultural labourer . . .

The 'glorious Revolution' brought into power, along with

William of Orange, the landlord and capitalist appropriators of surplus-value. They inaugurated the new era by practising on a colossal scale thefts of state lands, thefts that had been hitherto managed more modestly . . .

The last process of wholesale expropriation of the agricultural population from the soil is, finally, the so-called clearing of estates, i.e. the sweeping men off them. All the English methods hitherto considered culminated in 'clearing'. As we saw in the picture of modern conditions given in a former chapter, where there are no more independent peasants to get rid of, the 'clearing' of cottages begins; so that the agricultural labourers do not find on the soil cultivated by them even the spot necessary for their own housing . . .

The proletariat created by the breaking up of the bands of feudal retainers and by the forcible expropriation of the people from the soil, this 'free' proletariat could not possibly be absorbed by the nascent manufactures as fast as it was thrown upon the world. On the other hand, these men, suddenly dragged from their wonted mode of life, could not as suddenly adapt themselves to the discipline of their new condition. They were turned *en masse* into beggars, robbers, vagabonds, partly from inclination, in most cases from stress of circumstances. Hence at the end of the fifteenth and during the whole of the sixteenth century, throughout Western Europe a bloody legislation against vagabondage. The fathers of the present working class were chastised for their enforced transformation into vagabonds and paupers . . .

Thus were the agricultural people, first forcibly expropriated from the soil, driven from their homes, turned into vagabonds, and then whipped, branded, tortured by laws grotesquely terrible, into the discipline necessary for the wage system.

It is not enough that the conditions of labour are concentrated in a mass, in the shape of capital, at the one pole of society, while at the other are grouped masses of men, who have nothing to sell but their labour-power. Neither is it enough that they are compelled to sell it voluntarily. The advance of capitalist production develops a working class, which by education, tradition, habit, looks upon the conditions of that mode of production as self-evident laws of Nature . . .

The class of wage-labourers, which arose in the latter half of the fourteenth century, formed then and in the following century only a very small part of the population, well protected in its position by the independent peasant proprietary in the country and the guild-organization in the town . . .

The private property of the labourer in his means of production is the foundation of petty industry, whether agricultural, manufacturing, or both; petty industry, again, is an essential condition for the development of social production and of the free individuality of the labourer himself . . .

This mode of production presupposes parcelling of the soil, and scattering of the other means of production. . . . It is compatible only with a system of production, and a society, moving within narrow and more or less primitive bounds. . . . At a certain stage of development it brings forth the material agencies for its own dissolution. From that moment new forces and new passions spring up in the bosom of society; but the old social organization fetters them and keeps them down. It must be annihilated; it is annihilated. Its annihilation, the transformation of the individualized and scattered means of production into socially concentrated ones, of the pigmy property of the many into the huge property of the few, the expropriation of the great mass of the people from the soil, from the means of subsistence, and from the means of labour, this fearful and painful expropriation of the people forms the prelude to the history of capitalism.[72]

The proletariat goes through various stages of development. With its birth begins its struggle with the bourgeoisie. At first the contest is carried on by individual labourers, then by the workpeople of a factory, then by the operatives of one trade, in one locality, against the individual bourgeois who directly exploits them. They direct their attacks not against the bourgeois conditions of production, but against the instruments of production themselves; they destroy imported wares that compete with their labour, they smash to pieces machinery, they set factories ablaze, they seek to restore by force the vanished status of the workman of the Middle Ages.

At this stage the labourers still form an incoherent mass scattered over the whole country, and broken up by their mutual competition. . . . But with the development of industry the proletariat not only increases in number; it becomes concentrated in greater masses, its strength grows, and it feels that strength more . . . the collisions between individual workmen and individual bourgeois take more and more the character of collisions between two classes . . .

Now and then the workers are victorious, but only for a time. The real fruit of their battles lies, not in the immediate result, but in the ever-expanding union of the workers. . . . It was just this contact that was needed to centralize the numerous local struggles, all of the same character, into one national struggle between classes. But every class struggle is a political struggle . . .

This organization of the proletarians into a class, and consequently into a political party, is continually being upset again by the competition between the workers themselves. But it ever rises up again, stronger, firmer, mightier. It compels legislative recognition of particular interests of the workers, by taking advantage of the divisions among the bourgeoisie itself . . .

The advance of industry, whose involuntary promoter is the bourgeoisie, replaces the isolation of the labourers, due to competition, by their revolutionary combination, due to association. The development of Modern Industry, therefore, cuts from under its feet the very foundation on which the bourgeoisie produces and appropriates products. What the bourgeoisie, therefore, produces, above all, is its own grave-diggers.[73]

This view of Marx's of the development of modern classes, given here in an extremely compressed form, outlines the essential features of a class. But much of this view, even if we make allowances for the agitational nature of the Communist Manifesto, is not clearly defined.

The fifty-second chapter of Volume III of *Capital*, Marx's major work, was to be devoted to this problem. Only the beginning of the chapter was written; Marx died before he could complete it. The chapter is entitled 'Classes'.

The owners merely of labour-power, owners of capital, and land-owners, whose respective sources of income are wages, profit and ground-rent, in other words, wage-labourers, capitalists and land-owners, constitute the three big classes of modern society based upon the capitalist mode of production.

In England modern society is indisputably most highly and classically developed in economic structure. Nevertheless, even here the stratification of classes does not appear in its pure form. Middle and intermediate strata even here obliterate lines of demarcation everywhere (although incomparably less in rural districts than in the cities.) However, this is immaterial for our analysis . . .

The first question to be answered is this: What constitutes a class? – and the reply to this follows naturally from the reply to another question, namely: what makes wage-labourers, capitalist and landlords constitute the three great social classes?

At first glance – the identity of revenues and sources of revenue. There are three great social groups whose members, the individuals forming them, live on wages, profit and ground-rent respectively, on the realization of their labour-power, their capital and their landed property.

However, from this standpoint, physicians and officials, e.g., would also constitute two classes, for they belong to two distinct social groups, the members of each of these groups receiving their revenue from one and the same source. The same would also be true of the infinite fragmentation of interest and rank into which the division of social labour splits labourers as well as capitalists and landlords – the latter, e.g., into owners of vineyards, farm owners, owners of forests, mine owners and owners of fisheries.

(Here the manuscript breaks off.)[74]

This unfinished chapter is not the only place where Marx

draws attention to the multiple aspects of the division of labour and the multitude of 'middle and intermediate strata' which everywhere 'obliterate the lines of demarcation'.

Marx was not a lover of rigid formulas. He was an observer who never overlooked the individual and the specific in his search for general trends of social development. He did not view the crystallization of classes, highly resistant and effective social formations that they are, as a process tending towards a standstill. He always endeavoured to grasp it by taking into account the totality of its definitions.

In *The Eighteenth Brumaire of Louis Bonaparte*, one of his most brilliant works, he discusses such processes of change of the 'middle and intermediate strata'. As against the coalition of the bourgeoisie which had come into being shortly after the revolutionary events of 1848,

a coalition between petty bourgeois and workers had been formed, the so-called *social-democratic* party. The petty bourgeois saw that they were badly rewarded after the June days of 1848, that their material interests were imperilled and that the democratic guarantees which were to ensure the effectuation of these interests were called in question by the counter-revolution. Accordingly, they came closer to the workers. . . . From the social demands of the proletariat the revolutionary point was broken off and a democratic turn given to them; from the democratic claims of the petty bourgeoisie the purely political form was stripped off and their social point thrust forward. . . . The peculiar character of the Social-Democracy is epitomized in the fact that democratic – republican institutions are demanded as a means, not of doing away with two extremes, capital and wage labour, but of weakening their antagonism and transforming it into harmony.

The content of all the proposed measures 'is the transformation of society in a democratic way, but a transformation within the bounds of the petty bourgeoisie'.[75]

'The bourgeoisie now felt the necessity of making an end of the democratic petty bourgeois, just as a year before it had realized the necessity of settling with the revolutionary proletariat.' The 'party of Order' consciously conducts the class struggle.

But the democrat, because he represents the petty bourgeoisie, that is, a *transition class*, in which the interests of two classes are simultaneously mutually blunted, imagines himself elevated above class antagonism generally. The democrats concede that a privileged class confronts them, but they, along with all the rest of the nation, form the *people*.[76]

And if the bourgeoisie, which is consciously fighting for its class interests, is victorious, then that means that the people has 'failed' – or any other excuse – but it is never the admitted fault of the 'transition class' which wants to reconcile the irreconcilable, which has one foot on one side of the fence and one on the other, a class which is contradiction incarnate – in short, a class which has ceased to be one.

The phenomenon is even clearer in the case of the French small-holding peasants who supported Napoleon III as they had supported Napoleon I.

After the first revolution had transformed the peasants from semi-villeins into freeholders, Napoleon confirmed and regulated the conditions on which they could exploit undisturbed the soil of France which had only just fallen to their lot and slake their youthful passion for property. . . . The economic development of small-holding property has radically changed the relation of the peasants to the other classes of society. Under Napoleon the fragmentation of the land in the countryside supplemented free competition and the beginning of big industry in the towns. The peasant class was the ubiquitous protest against the landed aristocracy which had just been overthrown. . . . But in the course of the nineteenth century the feudal lords were replaced by urban usurers; the feudal obligation that went with the land was replaced by the mortgage; aristocratic landed property was replaced by bourgeois capital. . . . The interests of the peasants, therefore, are no longer, as under Napoleon, in accord with, but in opposition to the interests of the bourgeois order.[77]

The small-holding peasants form a vast mass, the members of which live in similar conditions but without entering into manifold relations with one another. . . . In so far as millions of families live under economic conditions of existence that separate their mode of life, their interests and their culture from those of the other classes, and put them in hostile opposition to the latter, they form a class. In so far as there is merely a local interconnexion among these small-holding peasants, and the identity of their interests begets no community, no national bond and no political organization among them, they do not form a class. They are consequently incapable of enforcing their class interest in their own name, whether through a parliament or through a convention. They cannot represent themselves, they must be represented. Their representative must at the same time appear as their master, as an authority over them, as an unlimited governmental power that protects them against the other classes and sends them rain and sunshine from above.[78]

Detailed analyses of this kind show why Marx refused to offer a simple definition or a ready-made formula in answer to the question: What is a class? They also show why he spoke of the 'great', the decisive, the historically determining classes of modern society.

Identity of revenues or of economic living conditions is not sufficient to constitute a social group as a class in the full sense of the word. A passive identity such as this, a community of interest dictated by destiny only, may be defined as a 'class in itself' (to use Hegelian terminology); it becomes a 'class for itself' only through a series of further determining circumstances, among which Marx counts the transcending of local limitations such as the individual factory, the individual community, the individual country – in other words, association and universality, the co-ordination and organization made possible thereby, the conscious opposition of the interests of one's own class to that of other classes, resistance, action, and the class struggle. *A class is born in the class struggle*. Only through such struggle does it develop into a social and historical force.

The position within the realm of socially necessary material production is of decisive importance, for without this realm society cannot exist. An army or a bureaucracy can enforce temporary decisions; but the structure of society and its relative stability are determined by groups directly concerned with the means of production, either as owners or as operators. In the process of technological development, small-scale private property of land, tools and materials is increasingly swallowed up by large-scale private property, so that classes of men such as artisans, small-holding peasants, the petty bourgeoisie are quite unable to hold their own as major classes conscious of a common purpose and engaged in a common fight; they refuse to recognize the polarization of society, feel themselves threatened both by capital and by the proletariat, are pulled this way and that on account of their contradictory economic interests, and tend, when the situation becomes critical, to call for a Napoleon, a strong man above the classes.

And so while Marx says that two great classes are increasingly alone in confronting one another – bourgeoisie and proletariat – he does not, when carrying out a concrete analysis, overlook the multitude of 'middle and intermediate' classes or the possibility of all kinds of alliances in the class struggle. The important thing is that more and more powerful means of production and more and more colossal capitals are concentrated in fewer and fewer hands, whilst on the other side the mass of those who own no means of production whatever and are forced to live by selling their labour power is growing incessantly: so that, overshadowing all else, *capital* and *labour* loom in opposition to one another.

From time to time, under special conditions, middle strata and intermediate classes are able to seize power – but never to retain it. The Jacobins, the party of the radical petty bourgeoisie, were replaced by the Directorate, the Directorate by Napoleon; and once more it was a Napoleon who, in the years after 1848, as the recognized guardian of the bourgeoisie, not only personified but also guaranteed the latter's dominance. Only the owners of massive means of production (land-owners, commercial magnates, industrialists and finance capitalists) can become a *ruling* class. However much the forms of their rule may differ from one another – ranging from the despotic to the democratic – this rule, whatever its form, is always based on their power over the means of production, on the institutions created for the protection of production relations, on the accustomed established order which comes to be thought of simply as 'order' (as though without it there would be chaos), on traditions, conventions, laws which confer the status of 'holy' and 'eternal' upon existing conditions. The ruling class needs an armed executive (and is prepared, in emergencies, to transfer dictatorial powers to that executive), but its principal power is the *objectified power* of the existing property and law relations.

The ideas of the ruling class are in every epoch the ruling ideas: i.e. the class, which is the ruling material force of society, is at the same time its ruling intellectual force. The class which has the means of material production at its disposal, has control at the same time over the means of mental production, so that thereby, generally speaking, the ideas of those who lack the means of mental production are subject to it. . . . The individuals composing the ruling class possess among other things consciousness, and therefore think. In so far, therefore, as they rule as a class and determine the extent and compass of an epoch, it is self-evident that they do this in their whole range, hence among other things rule also as thinkers, as producers of ideas, and regulate the production and distribution of the ideas of their age: thus their ideas are the ruling ideas of the epoch.[79]

The division of labour leads to a separation within the ruling class itself, namely as between those who *think* and those who *act*.

Within this class this cleavage can even develop into a certain opposition and hostility between the two parts, which, however, in the case of a practical collision, in which the class itself is endangered, automatically comes to nothing, in which case there also vanishes the semblance that the ruling ideas were not the ideas of the ruling class and had a power distinct from the power of this class. The existence of revolutionary ideas in a particular period presupposes the existence of a revolutionary class.[80]

Anti-intellectual circles within the labour movement often refer to this passage; but they are apt to overlook that, although 'in the case of a practical collision in which the class itself is endangered', the ideas of the ruling class will not contradict that class interest, the 'producers of ideas', that is to say the intellectuals, may disavow the ruling class and become its active opponents.

Finally, in times when the class struggle nears the decisive hour, the process of dissolution going on within the ruling class, in fact within the whole range of old society, assumes such a violent, glaring character, that a small section of the ruling class cuts itself adrift, and joins the revolutionary class, the class that holds the future in its hands. Just as, therefore, at an earlier period, a section of the nobility went over to the bourgeoisie, so now a portion of the bourgeoisie goes over to the proletariat, and in particular, a portion of the bourgeois ideologists, who have raised themselves to the level of comprehending theoretically the historical movement as a whole.[81]

More than that: those who have come into conflict with the rulers by reason of the very conditions of their existence rarely become a revolutionary *class* without the help of thinkers who, although they come from quite different spheres of society, 'have raised themselves to the level of comprehending theoretically the historical movement as a whole'. Marx and Engels were such thinkers.

The ruling class justifies its rule by claiming that it is the representative of law and order, of the moral principle; it claims that it does not rule as a class but as the defender of the 'common good':

The class making a revolution appears from the very start, merely because it is opposed to a *class*, not as a class but as the representative of the whole of society; it appears as the whole mass of society confronting the one ruling class. It can do this because, to start with, its interest really is more connected with the common interest of all other non-ruling classes, because under the pressure of conditions its interest has not yet been able to develop as the particular interest of a particular class. Its victory, therefore, benefits also many individuals of the other classes which are not winning a dominant position, but only in so far as it now puts these individuals in a position to raise themselves into a ruling class. When the French bourgeoisie overthrew the power of the aristocracy it thereby made it possible for many proletarians to raise themselves above the proletariat, but only in so far as they became bourgeois. Every new class, therefore, achieves its hegemony only on a broader basis than that of the class ruling previously, in return for which the opposition of the non-ruling class against the new ruling class later develops all the more sharply and profoundly. Both these things determine the fact that the struggle to be waged against this new ruling class, in its turn, aims at a more decided and radical negation of the previous conditions of society than could all previous classes which sought to rule.[82]

In this simplified exposé the fact that 'every new class

achieves its hegemony only on a broader basis than that of the class ruling previously' is mentioned only in passing. This 'broader basis' is an intrinsic element of progressive social development, and in another context Marx put the strongest emphasis on the historical achievement of the bourgeoisie and its role as constant revolutionizer of the state of the world. In the *Manifesto of the Communist Party* we read:

The bourgeoisie cannot exist without constantly revolutionizing the instruments of production, and thereby the relations of production, and with them the whole relations of society. Conservation of the old modes of production in unaltered form, was, on the contrary, the first condition of existence for all earlier industrial classes. Constant revolutionizing of production, uninterrupted disturbance of all social conditions, everlasting uncertainty and agitation distinguish the bourgeois epoch from all earlier ones. All fixed, fast-frozen relations, with their train of ancient and venerable prejudices and opinions, are swept away, all new-formed ones become antiquated before they can ossify. All that is solid melts into air, all that is holy is profaned, and man is at last compelled to face with sober senses, his real conditions of life, and his relations with his kind.[83]

The bourgeoisie has changed since then. At the time when the great capitalist monopolies were created it looked as though the bourgeoisie, turned reactionary, were neither able nor willing to carry on the continual revolutionizing of production, as though mankind were falling victim to an anti-rational ideology which would prevent man from 'facing with sober senses his relations with his kind'. And yet the continual revolutionizing of production (which attained unexampled scope during the scientific and technical revolution of our century), and the incessant change of all social conditions, has remained characteristic of the bourgeois era. It is precisely the international class struggle that keeps the bourgeoisie from becoming set in a rigid pattern.

The working class has changed too. In the advanced capitalist countries it is no longer the wretched proletariat of Marx's time; it has gained in size, differentiation, social status; it is becoming convinced of its ability to be the motive force of production and of social change. Many-layered and contradictory within itself, as a mass of wage and salary earners (workers, employees, technicians, engineers, administrators, scientists) it nevertheless represents an overwhelming majority over the owners of the means of production.

All previous historical movements were movements of minorities, or in the interest of minorities. The proletarian movement is the self-conscious, independent movement of the immense majority, in the interest of the immense majority. The proletariat, the lowest stratum of our present society, cannot stir, cannot raise itself up, without the whole superincumbent strata of official society being sprung into the air.[84]

Turns of phrase like 'sprung into the air' should not be taken literally. The basic thought, always recurring in Marx's work, was that the proletariat, which sets all the means of production in motion yet never owns them nor disposes of them, is the *last* class, a class that is constantly growing and is increasingly opposed to the division between labour and capital. In order to liberate itself as a class it must abolish the absurd conditions which make the only productive class of society the ruled class: it must abolish itself as a class, thus abolishing all classes and class rule as such.

In one of the most impressive passages in *Capital* Marx wrote:

Along with the constantly diminishing number of the magnates of capital . . . grows the mass of misery, oppression, slavery, degradation, exploitation; but with this too grows the revolt of the working class, a class always increasing in numbers, and disciplined, united, organized by the very mechanism of the process of capitalist production itself. The monopoly of production becomes a fetter upon the mode of production, which has sprung up and flourished along with, and under it. Centralization of the means of production and socialization of labour at last reach a point where they become incompatible with their capitalist integument. This integument is burst asunder. The knell of capitalist private property sounds. The expropriators are expropriated.[85]

Later on we shall inquire whether the 'mass of misery' has really grown. In the present context, the theory of classes and of the class struggle, which defines the revolutionary class in any given epoch as the pioneer of a new social era (until the creation of a classless and rulerless society), leads us directly to the philosophy of history developed by Marx and Engels: the philosophy of historical materialism.

6

HISTORICAL MATERIALISM

The capitalist mode of appropriation, the result of the capitalist mode of production, produces capitalist private property. This is the first negation of individual private property, as founded on the labour of the proprietor. But capitalist production begets, with the inexorability of a law of Nature, its own negation. It is the negation of negation. This does not re-establish private property for the producer, but gives him individual property based on the acquisitions of the capitalist era: i.e., on the co-operation and the possession in common of the land and of the means of production.[86]

In his *Preface to A Contribution to the Critique of Political Economy* Marx wrote – and his formulation has been repeated hundreds of times:

In the social production of their life men enter into definite relations that are indispensable and independent of their will, relations of production which correspond to a definite stage of development of their material productive forces. The sum total of these relations of production constitutes the economic structure of society, the real foundation, on which rises a legal and political superstructure and to which correspond definite forms of social consciousness. The mode of production of material life conditions the social, political and intellectual life process in general. It is not the consciousness of men that determines their being, but, on the contrary, their social being that determines their consciousness. At a certain stage of their development, the material productive forces of society come in conflict with the existing relations of production, or – what is but a legal expression for the same thing – with the property relations within which they have been at work hitherto. From forms of development of the productive forces these relations turn into their fetters. Then begins an epoch of social revolution. With the change of the economic foundation the entire immense superstructure is more or less rapidly transformed. In considering such transformations a distinction should always be made between the material transformation of the economic conditions of production, which can be determined with the precision of natural science, and the legal, political, religious, aesthetic of philosophic – in short, ideological forms in which men become conscious of this conflict and fight it out. Just as our opinion of an individual is not based on what he thinks of himself, so can we not judge of such a period of transformation by its own consciousness; on the contrary, this consciousness must be explained rather from the contradictions of material life, from the existing conflict between the social productive forces and the relations of production.[87]

The philosophy of history proposed here in concentrated form is an entirely new one. It views history neither as an accumulation of accidents, of the deeds of great men, nor as a process of constantly recurring ebbs and tides, an eternally self-repeating pattern – nor as the work of mysterious forces, predestined by some other-worldly plan of redemption or damnation or by the destiny of the World Spirit, but as the development of the human race determined by the nature of *labour*. The division of labour, the growth of productive forces, the association of production and private appropriation give rise, of necessity, to social contradictions. Every given stage of development of the productive forces requires certain specific forms of property, of relations between human beings and relations of production. Without such forms the productive forces cannot function and human society cannot exist. These forms correspond, first of all, to the level of the forces of production; but that level is never at a standstill; the development of the forces of production enters into manifold conflicts with the established relations of production, conflicts which could be resolved by mutual adaptation if antagonistic interests were not involved.

The growth of productive forces is inherent in the nature of labour. The possibility of satisfying not only elementary but even refined needs by the use of new tools, methods and knowledge demands its own realization, especially when the dynamic of capitalist production and competition has been set into motion. (In this connexion we should note that Marx draws a clear distinction between *private property* and *individual property*. Individual ownership of objects of necessity or luxury, of clothing, housing, furnishings, of articles of comfort rendered possible by technology, can be secured on the basis of co-operation and common ownership of the land and of the means of production created by labour itself. When Marx speaks of private property he means a form of property which, though social by its very nature, has been deprived of that social character by the affixing of an arbitrary sign which declares it to be *Private*.) Every mode of production carries its own negation within itself. The productive forces themselves burst the integument which is becoming a fetter upon them. A new order, adapted to the new forces of production, comes into being.

This fascinating theory of development of the human race which, though in no way predetermined, nevertheless obeys certain laws, is fraught with the danger of mechanical oversimplification, and it has not escaped that danger. Marx himself, great dialectician though he was, has on occasion provided future Marxists with an excuse for viewing history as an automatically functioning mechanism whose most important components are not living men but dead objects – instruments of labour, machines, object relations. Thus when he wrote, for example, of 'the advance of industry, whose involuntary promoter is the bourgeoisie'[88] (*Manifesto of the Communist Party*), or said that 'capitalist production begets, with the inexorability of a law of Nature, its own negation';[89] when, as he not infrequently did, he described society as 'a second Nature' subject to its own immutable natural laws – on these occasions he was unwittingly preparing the ground for oversimplification and misunderstandings.

We read in *The Poverty of Philosophy*:

Social relations are closely bound up with productive forces. In acquiring new productive forces men change their mode of production; and in changing their mode of production, in changing the way of earning their living, they change all their social relations. The hand-mill gives you society with the feudal lord; the steam-mill, society with the industrial capitalist.[90]

Many simplifiers of Marxist theory have deduced from this that the instruments of labour, not the men who use them, are the actual initiators and perpetrators of social change. In this way the productive forces have been *objectified*: once the steam-mill exists, what need is there for the class struggle of the bourgeoisie? And once we have got atomic power stations, surely the new society must come into being of its own accord? It is true that in the same *Poverty of Philosophy* we find a passage which reads:

Of all the instruments of production, the greatest productive power is the revolutionary class itself.[91]

And in *Wage Labour and Capital*, two years later, the same point is made more explicitly: 'A Negro is a Negro. He only becomes a slave in certain relations. A cotton-spinning jenny is a machine for spinning cotton. It becomes *capital* only in certain relations. Torn from these relationships it is no more capital than gold in itself is *money* or sugar the price of sugar.'[92]

In other words, the instruments of labour, the tools, machines and so forth, are only a part of the forces of production; men with their technical and social experience, their needs and their insights, the degree of their organization and consciousness, are more important. The steam-mill contributes towards creating a revolutionary class: but it is not the steam-mill that creates the revolutionary ideas which will grip the new class and make of it an active revolutionary class.

. . . But theory itself becomes a material force when it has seized the masses. Theory is capable of seizing the masses when it demonstrates *ad hominem*, and it demonstrates *ad hominem* as soon as it becomes radical. To be radical is to grasp things by the root. But for man the root is man himself.[93]

Certainly a revolutionary idea or theory can only seize the masses when the material pre-conditions for this have ripened with society. The root of man is man himself, but man under certain specific social conditions, not divorced from the totality of productive forces and production relations within which he is the conqueror or the victim, the hammer or the anvil. The works of man have become an alien power apparently independent from man himself, and these object relations follow certain laws which *resemble* the laws of nature; but they differ from them by the fact that the works of man did not make themselves, so that, although they may slip from the hands of their makers, they nevertheless continue to exercise an effect upon him, changing his capacities, his needs and his whole consciousness, and thus endowing him with the power to appropriate his own creation by transforming it in a revolutionary way.

Marx repeatedly compared the law of motion of history with natural laws, and his critics have repeatedly posed the question: If there is a historical law of development, what is the point of action and the class struggle? If a law of nature takes care of the sequence of social forms, why do we need political parties to organize the battle for socialism? The question is backed by a vulgarization of Marxism which has replaced the comparison between historical and natural laws by an identification of the two. In particular, Karl Kautsky, with his Darwinian background, did much to further the misunderstanding.

As we have already pointed out, there are passages in Marx which make such an interpretation possible. This can no doubt be explained by the influence of Hegel, who said of development that it maintains itself 'like an armoured phalanx' after the fashion of 'the sun in its course'; and Darwin's theory of evolution also had a lasting influence on Marx, who saw in it a direct confirmation of laws of development.

In some passages too much stress is laid on the works of man and too little on man himself and on his interaction with the social world he has created and which has grown beyond his control:

Although, then, the whole of this movement appears as a social process, and although the separate elements of this movement derive from the conscious will and specific aims of individuals, the totality of the process nevertheless appears as an objective relationship which comes into being naturally: emerging from the clash between conscious individuals, but being neither contained within their consciousness nor subsumed as a whole under them. Their mutual clashes produce a social power which stands above them and is alien to them; their interaction is a process and a force independent of themselves.[94]

However, close study of such passages in conjunction with the overall concept of historical materialism shows that, while Marx occasionally over-emphasized the 'natural laws' of historical development, he never overlooked the fact that it is men themselves who make their history, even in a world of alienation in which the products of human activity have assumed a ghostly life of their own.

In an article on *The Future Results of British Rule in India,* written on 22 July 1853, this differentiation between the 'natural law' which governs society and the activity of revolutionary movements which alter the laws of previous developments is made patently clear.

After describing the 'devastating' effects of English industry on India, Marx writes:

Bourgeois industry and commerce create these material conditions of a new world in the same way as geological revolutions have created the surface of the earth. When a great social revolution shall have mastered the results of the bourgeois epoch, the market of the world and the modern powers of production, and subjected them to the common control of the most advanced peoples, then only will human progress cease to resemble that hideous pagan idol, who would not drink the nectar but from the skulls of the slain.[95]

The passage is of interest not only because it confirms that Marx expected the victory of the socialist revolution to occur more or less simultaneously in the industrially developed countries, and not only because it proves that Marx had left Hegel's idea of a regular and continuous development behind him. It is above all significant in the present context because here the comparison with natural law goes hand in hand with the recognition of a conscious activity of conscious forces.

The same meaning emerges from the 'Afterword' to the second edition of *Capital*, where Marx quotes with approval the following text by a Russian commentator:

As soon as society has outlived a given period of development, and is passing over from one given stage to another, it begins to be subject also to other laws. In a word, economic life offers us a phenomenon analogous to the history of evolution in other branches of biology. The old economists misunderstood the nature of economic laws when they likened them to the laws of physics and chemistry. . . . With the varying degree of development of productive power, social conditions and the laws governing them vary too.[96]

Marx's concept of history as a whole was based on the conviction that there exists an *objective* development containing within it the formation of a *subjective* factor which is then instrumental in realizing the development. Private property

drives itself in its economic movement towards its own dissolution, only, however, through a development which does not depend on it, of which it is unconscious and which takes place against its will, through the very nature of things; only inasmuch as it produces the proletariat *as* proletariat, that misery conscious of its spiritual and physical misery, that dehumanization conscious of its dehumanization and therefore self-abolishing.[97]

The belief in the necessity of development contains within it the belief that an ever-increasing number of human beings will effect the necessary development by free decision. This is not, as Marx's critics often claim, the fundamental contradiction of Marxism: it is the *fundamental idea of Marxist dialectics*.

In our opinion Marx never abandoned the view he proclaimed in *The Holy Family*:

History does *nothing*, it 'possesses *no* immense wealth', it 'wages *no* battles'. It is *man*, real living man, that does all that, that possesses and fights; 'history' is not a person apart, using man as means for its own particular aims; history is *nothing but the activity of man pursuing his aims*.[98]

Being not just a socialist thinker, but also a leader of the labour movement, Marx was fully aware of the need to organize those forces whose interest it is to advance a development recognized as necessary:

The political movement of the working class has as its ultimate object, of course, the conquest of political power for the working class, and for this it is naturally necessary that a previous organization of the working class, arising from its economic struggles, should have been developed up to a certain point . . .

Where the working class is not yet far enough advanced in its organization to undertake a decisive campaign against the collective power, that is, the political power, of the ruling classes, it must at any rate be trained for this by continual agitation against the policy of the ruling classes and adopting an attitude hostile to it. Otherwise it will remain a plaything in their hands . . .[99]

That is why we find in Marx, side by side with comparisons with natural history whose purpose was doubtless to draw attention to the novelty of his theory, clear indications that he meant social and historical laws to be understood as *laws having the character of tendencies*.

Under capitalist production, the general law acts as the prevailing tendency only in a very complicated and approximate manner, as a never ascertainable average of ceaseless fluctuations.[100]

A passage from a letter to Dr Ludwig Kugelmann of 17 April 1871 shows how little inclined Marx was to compare historical development with Hegel's 'sun in its course':

World history would indeed be very easy to make, if the struggle were taken up only on condition of infallibly favourable chances. It would, on the other hand, be of a very mystical nature, if 'accidents' played no part. These accidents themselves fall naturally into the general course of development and are compensated again by other accidents. But acceleration and delay are very dependent upon such 'accidents', which include the 'accident' of the character of those who at first stand at the head of the movement.[101]

Even laws of nature are only an expression of maximum probability. The laws of social movement have the character of tendencies. What happens does not have to have happened.

In *The Eighteenth Brumaire of Louis Bonaparte* Marx analyses in great detail the social situation and the economic and class pre-conditions for an adventurer's rise to dictatorship:

It is not enough to say, as the French do, that their nation was taken unawares. A nation and a woman are not forgiven the unguarded hour in which the first adventurer that comes along could violate them. . . . It remains to be explained how a nation of thirty-six millions can be surprised and delivered unresisting into captivity by three high-class swindlers.[102]

The explanation is supplied with a natural scientist's precision. But then Marx goes on to describe Napoleon's political defeat of 10 March 1850, adding:

The party of Order proved unable to take advantage of this opportunity that would never return. Instead of boldly possessing itself of the power offered, it did not even compel Bonaparte to reinstate the ministry dismissed on November 1. . . . The social-democratic party, for its part, seemed only to try to find pretexts for putting its own victory once again in doubt and for blunting its point. . . . Instead of . . . forcing the adversary to fight at the moment of popular enthusiasm and favourable mood in the army, the democratic party wearied Paris during the months of March and April with a new election campaign, let the aroused popular passions wear themselves out in this repeated provisional election game, let the revolutionary energy satiate itself with constitutional successes, dissipate itself in petty intrigues, hollow declamations and sham movements.[103]

We see that Marx analyses not only the laws of the development but also those situations in which an alternative offered itself. Similarly we may say that the tendency towards fascism during the years of the great slump was immensely strong, yet Hitler's triumph was by no means due to a social 'law of nature'. Marx's philosophy of history is not historical fatalism; it does not exclude the alternative; from the fact that *decisions are conditioned*, it does not deduce that *destiny is unconditional*.

Like the problem of the laws of development, the mutual relationship between 'basis' and 'superstructure' has been mechanically misunderstood not only by Marx's critics but also by many of his followers; and the misunderstanding still continues.

Intellectual production does not follow material production but occurs simultaneously and in constant interaction with it. What emerges as the 'superstructure' is a totality of prescriptions and prohibitions, laws, institutions, judgements and prejudices which corresponds to the economic structure of society, the degree of division of labour and the interests of the class which, by reason of the division of labour, has become the ruling class at that time. Hence the ideas of the rulers are the dominant ideas, but not the only ones, of the epoch. Marx stressed again and again that every new society carries its own negation within itself, the inner contradiction which finds its most striking expression in the class struggle. Every new society is therefore the negation of the preceding one, whose habits, ideas and notions continue to exist deep within it. 'The tradition of all the dead generations weighs like a nightmare on the brain of the living.'[104]

And at the same time the future society ripens as a negation inside the existing one, conditioned by the growth of the material and spiritual forces of production. Thus the dominant ideas are always permeated by other, rebellious ones, which may be forward or backward-looking, so that the class struggle is fought not only as an economic but also as a political and intellectual battle. Marx and Engels repeatedly denied that economic conditions and demands, although 'in the last instance' primary, should be seen as the *only* historical driving forces; they denied that *every* historical movement, *every* political event, *every* philosophic idea must be directly and exclusively ascribed to economic processes.

And so the architectural concept of 'basis' and 'super-structure' should not lead to the notion that society is like a building of which first the economic foundations must be laid (in the hope, perhaps, that the stones will arrange themselves into a 'basis' of their own accord), to be followed by the superstructure, one floor succeeding the next all the way up to the roof, as if in obedience to the law of gravity and the architect's command. Only a parrot schoolboy utterly devoid of imagination can get by with the ever-available quotation that social being determines consciousness and not the other way about. Whenever he analysed a concrete political situation Marx made it clear that social being is more than just the sum of economic conditions. Conditions are affected by many elements of consciousness – true, false or clouded consciousness. Since men are beings endowed with consciousness there is no rigid frontier between consciousness and social being. The essential thing about the philosophy of history developed by Marx is that it always proceeds from *social reality*, not from abstract categories: from the 'simple material production of life', not from intellectual constructs: from practice, not from a set of self-generating, self-developing, self-resolved ideas.

Our conception of history depends on our ability to expound the real process of production, starting out from the simple material production of life, and to comprehend the form of intercourse* connected with this and created by this (i.e. civil society in its various stages), as the basis of all history; further, to show it in its action as State; and so, from this starting-point, to explain the whole mass of different theoretical products and forms of consciousness, religion, philosophy, ethics, etc., etc., and trace their origins and growth, by which means, of course,

* *Author's note:* In later works Marx replaced this concept by that of 'production relations'.

the whole thing can be shown in its totality (and therefore, too, the reciprocal action of these various sides on one another). It has not, like the idealistic view of history, in every period to look for a category, but remains constantly on the real ground of history. . . . It shows that history does not end by being resolved into 'self-consciousness' as 'spirit of the spirit', but that in it at each stage there is found a material result: a sum of productive forces, a historically created relation of individuals to nature and to one another, which is handed down to each generation from its predecessor; a mass of productive forces, different forms of capital, and conditions, which, indeed, is modified by the new generation on the one hand, but also on the other prescribes for it its conditions of life and gives it a definite development, a special character. It shows that circumstances make men just as much as men make circumstances.[105]

In the *Theses on Feuerbach* Marx's polemic against the shortcomings of previous materialist doctrine which overlooked the active side of man and ignored human *practice* as the world-changing activity, Marx repeats the same thought:

The materialistic doctrine concerning the changing of circumstances and education forgets that circumstances are changed by men and that the educator himself must be educated . . . The coincidence of the changing of circumstances and of human activity or self-changing can only be comprehended and rationally understood as *revolutionary practice*.[106]

Revolutionary practice changes circumstances and changes man himself. It sees man not only as the object of history but also as its subject: he is an object capable, by subjective activity, of becoming a subject and of changing existing circumstances. It is in the recognition of this constant inter-action between man and his works, between social 'laws of nature' and the nature of man as a being capable of changing the circumstances he finds around him, between production relations which tend to conserve what has already been achieved and material and intellectual productive forces which press inexorably forward, that we find the quintessence and the culmination of historical materialism.

Men make their own history, but they do not make it just as they please; they do not make it under circumstances chosen by themselves, but under circumstances directly encountered, given and transmitted from the past.[107]

7

VALUE AND SURPLUS VALUE

Even the most simplified summary of the economic ideas Marx developed in *Capital* – his major work – as well as in *Wages, Price and Profit, Foundations of the Critique of Political Economy, A Contribution to the Critique of Political Economy, Theories of Surplus Value, Wage Labour and Capital* and in many other writings, would require a separate book in itself, not to mention the many and complex objections to these ideas raised by Marx's critics and the replies given, in part, by Marx himself in anticipation of such criticisms. We are obliged in this chapter to confine ourselves to formulating and explaining a few basic concepts, most of which we have already had occasion to touch upon in earlier chapters.

We remind our readers of Chapter 4 ('The Fetish Character of the Commodity') and repeat: Every commodity must first of all satisfy a need; it must be useful; that is to say, it must have a *use-value*.

In a developed system of commodity exchange it is found that useful objects – use-values – are mutually exchangeable, not in an arbitrary manner but in accordance with a *measure* or law common to all objects once they have been transformed into commodities. Although fluctuations are unavoidable because of excessive or insufficient supply, price pushing, speculation, etc., these fluctuations nevertheless occur around a certain magnitude which always asserts itself as the secret of the object-as-commodity.

Marx points out that Aristotle already saw the exchange of commodities in accordance with a certain measure – a simple and natural thing on the face of it – as something highly enigmatic.

' "Exchange", he says, "cannot take place without equality, and equality not without commensurability." Here, however, he comes to a stop, and gives up the further analysis of the form of value. "It is, however, in reality, impossible that such unlike things can be commensurable" – i.e., qualitatively equal. Such an equalization can only be something foreign to their real nature, consequently only "a makeshift for practical purposes".' And Marx provides the answer: the 'common substance' Aristotle looked for but failed to find is *human labour*.

There was, however, an important fact which prevented Aristotle from seeing that, to attribute value to commodities, is merely a mode of expressing all labour as equal human labour, and consequently as labour of equal quality. Greek society was founded upon slavery, and had, therefore, for its natural basis, the inequality of men and of their labour-powers. The secret of the expression of value, namely, that all kinds of labour are equal and equivalent, and so far as they are human labour in general, cannot be deciphered, until the notion of human equality has already acquired the fixity of a popular prejudice. This, however, is possible only in a society in which the great mass of the produce of labour takes the form of commodities, in which, consequently, the dominant relation between man and man is that of owners of commodities.[108]

When we speak of the value of a commodity, then, we mean its exchange value. The value of a coat is greater than that of the fabric of which it is made, the value of the fabric greater than that of the wool, yarn, natural or artificial fibre of which it consists. This value increase can only be explained by the fact that something has been added at every stage: yet nothing has been added except human labour. It is by the quantity of labour involved that the value of a commodity is measured; and the quantity itself is measured by the time spent on labour.

Some people might think that if the value of a commodity is determined by the quantity of labour spent on it, the more idle and unskilful the labourer, the more valuable would his commodity be, because more time would be required in its production. The labour, however, that forms the substance of value, is homogeneous human labour, expenditure of one uniform labour-power. The total labour-power of society, which is embodied in the sum total of the values of all commodities produced by that society, counts here as one homogeneous mass of human labour-power, composed though it be of innumerable individual units. Each of these units is the same as any other, so far as it has the character of the average labour-power of society, and takes effect as such; that is, so far as it requires for producing a commodity, no more time than is needed on an average, no more than is socially necessary.[109]

'The value of one commodity is to the value of any other, as the labour-time necessary for the production of the one is to that necessary for the production of the other.' Having said this, Marx immediately re-formulates it in a more striking form: 'As values, all commodities are only definite masses of congealed labour-time'.[110] The image does not merely suggest how living labour congeals into a dead object: the association with dripping sweat and congealed blood is almost inescapable.

Is, then, every kind of labour equal to every other kind – skilled labour to unskilled, simple labour to that which presupposes specialized knowledge? Marx distinguishes between *simple average labour* which, though it changes its character from one country and one culture to another, is nevertheless a given thing in any existing society, and *skilled labour*.

But

skilled labour counts only as simple labour intensified, or rather, as multiplied simple labour, a given quantity of skilled being considered equal to a greater quantity of simple labour. Experience shows that this reduction is constantly being made.[111] . . . All labour of a higher or more complicated character than average labour is expenditure of labour-power of a more costly kind, labour-power whose production has cost more time and labour, and which therefore has a higher value, than unskilled or simple labour-power.[112]

Developed commodity exchange demands a universal equivalent, a commodity which serves as the standard for all commodities and, as such, acquires 'real consistence and general social validity'. Gold and silver – money – have been made into this universal equivalent.[113]

Money is a crystal formed of necessity in the course of the exchanges, whereby different products of labour are practically equated to one another and thus by practice converted into commodities. The historical progress and extension of exchanges develops the contrast, latent in commodities, between use-value and value.[114]

Use-value becomes the determining value only in extreme situations; as a general rule, it is exchange value which – as 'congealed labour-time' – makes up the value of a commodity.

The *value* of a commodity is not identical with its *price*; but prices are connected, however elastically, with value, circling it as electrons circle the nucleus of the atom.

Socially necessary labour of equal magnitude can be expressed by different prices. These prices may be

too small or too great properly to express the magnitude of the wheat's value, nevertheless they are its prices, for they are, in the first place, the form under which its value appears, i.e. money; and in the second place, the exponents of its exchange-ratio with money . . . But this exchange-ratio may express either the real magnitude of that commodity's value, or the quantity of gold deviating from that value, for which, according to circumstances, it may be parted with. The possibility, therefore, of quantitative incongruity between price and magnitude of value, or the deviation of the former from the latter, is inherent in the price-form itself. This is no defect, but, on the contrary, admirably adapts the price-form to a mode or production whose inherent laws impose themselves only as the mean of apparently lawless irregularities that compensate one another.[115]

Here a comparison with natural science is not out of place. The rule of molecular movement exists only as a blindly arbitrary average rule of lawlessness. In production, the social character of the production process asserts itself as the value of the commodity determined by the quantity of socially necessary labour-time; the price expresses the accidental nature of the market and the planlessness of an economy based purely on profit.

A rise or fall in the prices of a number of leading articles is sufficient in the one case to increase, in the other to diminish, the sum of the prices of all commodities, and, therefore, to put more or less money in circulation. Whether the change in the price corresponds to an actual change of value in the commodities, or whether it be the result of mere fluctuations in market-prices, the effect on the quantity of the medium of circulation remains the same.[116]

The three factors which determine the market are: state of prices, quantity of circulating commodities, and velocity of money-currency. These factors 'are all variable. Hence the sum of the prices to be realized, and consequently the quantity of the circulating medium depending on that sum, will vary with the numerous variations of these three factors.'[117]

A slow historical process turns *money* into *capital*. As such, money gains a dynamic force and is no longer simply a means of payment, of spending, of saving or usury, not only a measure of value, but the *motive force of production.*

The circulation of commodities is the starting-point of capital. The production of commodities, their circulation, and that more developed form of their circulation called commerce, these form the historical ground-work from which it rises. The modern history of capital dates from the creation in the sixteenth century of a world-embracing commerce and a world-embracing market.[118]

The simple circulation of commodities – selling in order to buy – is a means of carrying out a purpose unconnected with circulation, namely, the appropriation of use-values, the satisfaction of wants. The circulation of money as capital is, on the contrary, an end in itself, for the expansion of value takes place only within this constantly renewed movement. The circulation of capital has therefore no limits.[119]

In simple commodity exchange the use-value predominates. Whoever sells his product wants to buy another with the money he has made. A demand for a concrete object is satisfied on both sides. But for the capitalist the object produced is a matter of indifference. He merely wants to turn his commodity, whatever it may be, into money. He wants to get more money out of it than he has put into it. The product he sells must be so constituted that a part of the value that has accrued to it through labour will fall into his hands.

The expansion of value . . . becomes his subjective aim, and it is only in so far as the appropriation of even more and more wealth in the abstract becomes the sole motive of his operations that he functions as a capitalist, that is, as capital personified and endowed with consciousness and a will. Use-values must therefore never be looked upon as the real aim of the capitalist; neither must the profit on any single transaction. The restless never-ending process of profit-making alone is what he aims at. This boundless greed after riches, this passionate chase after exchange-value, is common to the capitalist and the miser; but while the miser is merely a capitalist gone mad, the capitalist is a rational miser. The never-ending augmentation of exchange-value, which the miser strives after by seeking to save his money from circulation, is attained by the more acute capitalist, by constantly throwing it afresh into circulation.[120]

How can the capitalist 'expand' value and get more value for himself in proportion as he puts more value on the market? Occasionally he can do this by outwitting his fellow business-men or as a result of price fluctuations and money speculation. But in the long run there must be some means that is available to all capitalists, some commodity

whose use-value possesses the peculiar property of being a source of value, whose actual consumption, therefore, is itself an embodiment of labour and, consequently, a creation of value. The possessor of money does find on the market such a special commodity in capacity for labour or labour-power.[121]

Labour-power

can appear upon the market as a commodity, only if, and so far as, its possessor, the individual whose labour-power it is, offers it for sale, or sells it, as a commodity. In order that he may be able to do this, he must have it at his disposal, must be the untrammelled owner of his capacity for labour, i.e. of his person. . . . For the conversion of his money into capital, there-fore, the owner of money must meet in the market with the free labourer, free in the double sense, that as a free man he can dispose of his labour-power as his own commodity, and that on the other hand he has no other commodity for sale, is short of everything necessary for the realization of his labour-power.[122]

This peculiar commodity, labour-power, has its value like all other commodities. But how is this value determined?

The value of labour-power is determined, as in the case of

every other commodity, by the labour-time necessary for the production, and consequently also the reproduction, of this special article. So far as it has value, it represents no more than a definite quantity of the average labour of society incorporated in it. . . . Given the individual, the production of labour-power consists in his reproduction of himself or his maintenance. For his maintenance he requires a given quantity of the means of subsistence. Therefore the labour-time requisite for the production of labour-power reduces itself to that necessary for the production of those means of subsistence; in other words, the value of labour-power is the value of the means of subsistence necessary for the maintenance of the labourer.[123]

The minimum limit of the value of labour-power is determined by the value of the commodities, without the daily supply of which the labourer cannot renew his vital energy, consequently by the value of those means of subsistence that are physically indispensable. If the price of labour-power falls to this minimum, it falls below its value, since under such circumstances it can be maintained and developed only in a crippled state. But the value of every commodity is determined by the labour-time requisite to turn it out so as to be of normal quality.

It is a very cheap sort of sentimentality which declares this method of determining the value of labour-power, a method prescribed by the very nature of the case, to be a brutal method.[124]

This rejection of cheap sentimentality, the hard matter-of-factness with which Marx speaks of labour-power as a commodity having a value and a price like any other, reveals more tellingly than any excess of feeling the viciousness of a system in which man is turned into a commodity like any dead product and the labour-time necessary for its reproduction becomes the value of that commodity. Marx, who was capable of such passion and pathos as an accuser, here does justice to the *dehumanization of man* in the world in which he lived by using the language of *objectification*.

Marx supposes that the value of a day's labour amounts to 3

shillings. Half a day's labour is embodied in that quantity of labour-power, because the means of subsistence that are daily required for the production of labour-power cost half a day's labour. But the past labour that is embodied in labour-power and the living labour that it can perform, the daily cost of maintaining labour-power and its own daily expenditure in work are two totally different things. The former determines the exchange-value of labour-power, the latter its use-value.

The fact that half a day's labour is necessary to keep the labourer alive during 24 hours does not in any way prevent him from working a whole day. Therefore the value of labour-power, and the value which that labour-power creates in the labour-process, are two entirely different magnitudes; and this difference of the two values was what the capitalist had in view, when he was purchasing the labour-power . . .

Our capitalist foresaw this state of things, and that was the cause of his laughter. The labourer therefore finds, in the workshop, the means of production necessary for working, not only during 6, but during 12 hours. Just as during the six hours' process our 10 lb. of cotton absorbed 6 hours' labour, and became 10 lb. of yarn, so now 20 lb. of cotton will absorb 12 hours' labour and be changed into 20 lb. of yarn. Let us now examine the product of this prolonged process. There is now materialized in this 20 lb. of yarn the labour of five days, of which four days are due to the cotton and the lost steel of the spindle, the remaining day having been absorbed by the cotton during the spinning process. Expressed in gold, the labour of five days is thirty shillings. This is therefore the price of the 20 lb. of yarn. . . . But the sum of the values of the commodities that entered into the process amounts to 27 shillings. The value of the yarn is 30 shillings. Therefore the value of the product is $\frac{1}{9}$ greater than the value advanced for its production; 27 shillings have been transformed into 30 shillings; a surplus value of 3 shillings has been created. . . . Money has been converted into capital.[125]

To the usual objection that the capitalist also works and thereby contributes to the formation of value we may advance the question: What do capitalists live on whose only activity consists in cashing dividends? It is quite evident that workers, technicians, engineers and so forth perform *surplus labour*, a part of which becomes the revenue or income of one or several owners. If it were not for this surplus value the money the owners put in their pockets would have to be considered a free gift which the workers granted them out of pure Christian charity – a likely story!

True, the *product of labour* acquires part of its value from the *instrument of labour*, in which past labour is accumulated. What the product acquires, the instrument loses in terms of its use-value.

If such an instrument has no value to lose, if, in other words, it is not the product of human labour, it transfers no value to the product. It helps to create use-value without contributing to the formation of exchange-value. In this class are included all means of production supplied by Nature without human assistance, such as land, wind, water, metals in situ, and timber in virgin forests.[126]

. . . The means of production transfer value to the new product, so far only as during the labour-process they lose value in the shape of their old use-value. The maximum loss of value that they can suffer in the process, is plainly limited by the amount of the original value with which they came into the process, or in other words, by the labour-time necessary for their production.[127]

The surplus of the total value of the product over the sum of values of its component elements (raw and auxiliary materials, instruments of labour and human labour-power) is thus obtained solely from the human labour-power which expends more labour-time than is necessary for its maintenance. That part of capital which is invested in the means of production does not change in value during the production process. Marx calls this *constant capital*.

On the other hand, that part of capital, represented by labour-power, does, in the process of production, undergo an alteration of value. It both reproduces the equivalent of its own value, and also produces an excess, a surplus-value, which may itself vary, may be more or less according to circumstances. This part of capital is continually being transformed from a constant into a variable magnitude. I therefore call it the variable part of capital, or, shortly, *variable capital*.[128]

The labour-power which the worker expends beyond the labour necessary for his maintenance creates no value *for him*. It creates *surplus value*, which for the capitalist, as Marx puts it, 'has all the charm of a creation out of nothing'.[129]

The relationship between capitalist and worker presupposes a struggle from the outset: struggle for the *rate of surplus value*, i.e. the proportion of surplus labour-time to that labour-time necessary for the maintenance of labour-power – in other words, first and foremost, for the length of the working-day. The worker does not merely, like an animal, need a part of the day in order to rest, eat and satisfy his physical requirements.

The labourer needs time for satisfying his intellectual and social wants, the extent and number of which are conditioned by the general state of social advancement. The variation of the working-day fluctuates, therefore, within physical and social bounds.[130]

What is a working-day? How much shorter should it be than a natural living day? The capitalist's view concerning the necessary limitation of the working-day differs from the worker's.

As capitalist he is only capital personified. . . . But capital has one single life impulse, the tendency to create value and surplus-value, to make its constant factor, the means of production, absorb the greatest possible amount of surplus-labour. Capital is dead labour, that, vampire-like, only lives by sucking living labour, and lives the more, the more labour it sucks. The time during which the labourer works, is the time during which the capitalist consumes the labour-power he has purchased of him. If the labourer consumes his disposable time for himself, he robs the capitalist.[131]

It would be quite wrong to imagine that Marx considered every capitalist to be a villain or a rogue. He did not see the capitalist as an individual but only as a 'social character mask', a 'functionary of capital', who, by virtue of the law of commodity exchange, demands the full value of the commodity he has purchased.

The capitalist maintains his right as a purchaser when he tries to make the working-day as long as possible, and to make, whenever possible, two working-days out of one. On the other hand, the peculiar nature of the commodity sold implies a limit to its consumption by the purchaser, and the labourer maintains his right as seller when he wishes to reduce the working-day to one of definite normal duration. There is here, therefore, an antinomy, right against right, both equally bearing the seal of the law of exchanges. Between equal rights force decides. Hence is it that in the history of capitalist production, the determination of what is a working-day, presents itself as the result of a struggle, a struggle between collective capital, i.e. the class of capitalists, and collective labour, i.e. the working class.[132]

With great matter-of-factness as well as passion, Marx described the progress of this struggle for the 'normal working-day', particularly in England, as a struggle in which the labourers were able to win certain victories within the capitalist system, but in which, at the same time, they became aware of the limitations of that system based on the buying and selling of human labour-power – on surplus labour, not in the service of the community, but for private interest.*

* The fact that Marx foresaw the age of automation and, with it, the necessity to modify the theory of surplus value, testifies to his greatness as a thinker. In the *Foundations of the Critique of Political Economy* he wrote:

To the extent that large-scale industry is developed, the creation of real wealth comes to depend less and less on the labour time and the quantum of labour employed compared with the power of the agents set in motion during that labour time, which in its turn – in its *powerful effectiveness* – is not minimally related to the immediate labour time that their production costs, but depends rather on the general state of science and of the progress of technology, or of the application of this science to production. . . . Work no longer seems to be included in the production process as man rather stands apart from the production process as its regulator and guardian. . . . He stands beside the production process rather than being its principal agent. In this transformation it is less the immediate labour performed by man himself or the time that he works than the appropriation of his general productivity, his comprehension of nature and dominion over it through his existence as a social body – in a word, the development of the social individual – that appears as the supporting pillar of production and wealth. The theft of the labour time of others on which wealth is based today appears as a miserable basis compared with the new basis which has developed in the meanwhile, created by a large-scale industry itself. Hardly has labour in an immediate form ceased to be the major source of wealth than labour time ceases, and must cease, to be its measure, and thus exchange-value the measure of use-value. The surplus labour of the masses has ceased to be the condition for the development of general wealth, just as the non-labour of the few has ceased to be the condition for the development of the general forces of the human mind. Thus production based on exchange-value crumbles . . . (*Marx's Notes on Machines*. Translated by Ben Brewster. Sublation Offprint No. 1, *Sublation*, Students' Union, Leicester University, Leicester, 6 December 1966, pp. 14–16.)

8

PROFIT AND CAPITAL

When value leaves the sphere of production, in which it originates, and enters that of the market, of commerce and circulation, it becomes *price*; as such, as we have seen, it also becomes more indefinite, more capricious, more readily influenced by a variety of circumstances. Value as price follows an adventurous course, especially when a sudden price drop reveals one of the secrets of the capitalist mode of production: namely, that production is, in principle, limitless and without measure, whereas consumption is limited by demand and purchasing power.

Something similar happens to *surplus value* when it leaves the sphere of production – in which alone it, too, has its origin – in order to reappear as *profit* in the sphere of the market, of distribution and sale. The cost-price of a commodity (i.e. the total sum expended on its production) is lower than its value. Commodity value = cost-price + profit.

Hence, if a commodity is sold at its value, a profit is realized which is equal to the excess of its value over its cost-price, and therefore equal to the entire surplus-value incorporated in the value of the commodity. But the capitalist may sell a commodity at a profit even when he sells it below its value. So long as its selling-price is higher than its cost-price, though it may be lower than its value, a portion of the surplus-value incorporated in it is always realized, thus always yielding a profit.[133]

Marx dismisses as a 'thoughtless conception' the idea that

the cost-price of a commodity constitutes its actual value, and that surplus-value springs from selling the product above its value, so that commodities would be sold at their value if their selling-price were to equal their costing-price, i.e. if it were to equal the price of the consumed means of production plus wages.[134]

Surplus value is exclusively the result of living labour-power, of surplus labour, of the exploitation of the workers. The rate of surplus value – the proportion of surplus labour time to necessary labour time – therefore relates to variable capital only. Profit, on the other hand, relates to the total capital, both variable and constant. Hence the rate of profit is also the proportion of the sale price to the cost price.

The rate of surplus-value measured against the variable capital is called rate of surplus-value. The rate of surplus-value measured against the total capital is called rate of profit. These are two different measurements of the same entity, and owing to the difference of the two standards of measurement they express different proportions or relations of this entity.

The transformation of surplus-value into profit must be deduced from the transformation of the rate of surplus-value into the rate of profit, not vice versa. And in fact it was rate of profit which was the historical point of departure. Surplus-value and rate of surplus-value are, relatively, the invisible and unknown essence that wants investigating, while rate of profit and therefore the appearance of surplus-value in the form of profit are revealed on the surface of the phenomenon.[135]

Although the rate of profit thus differs numerically from the rate of surplus-value, while surplus-value and profit are actually the same thing and numerically equal, profit is nevertheless a converted form of surplus-value, a form in which its origin and the secret of its existence are obscured and extinguished. In effect, profit is the form in which surplus-value presents itself to the view, and must initially be stripped by analysis to disclose the latter. In surplus-value, the relation between capital and labour is laid bare; in the relation of capital to profit, i.e. of capital to surplus-value that appears on the one hand as an excess over the cost-price of commodities realized in the process of circulation and, on the other, as a surplus more closely determined by its relation to the total capital, the capital appears as a *relation to itself*, a relation in which it, as the original sum of value, is distinguished from a new value which it generated.[136]

The rate of profit is related to the rate of surplus-value as the variable capital is to the total capital.[137]

Thus the level of the rate of profit is dependent not only on that of the rate of surplus value, but also on the composition of the capital and its speed of circulation; but the fact that there can be profit at all is determined only by surplus labour, which creates surplus value. Although the two rates appear in different form, their intrinsic nature is the same.

As already pointed out,

Capitalist production is in itself indifferent to the particular use-value and distinctive features of any commodity it produces. In every sphere of production it is only concerned with producing surplus-value, and appropriating a certain quantity of unpaid labour incorporated in the product of labour.[138]

To the individual capitalist, however, the production process need by no means appear simply as a process of the production of surplus value. The capitalist may feel himself to be a captain of industry, not merely an exploiter of men. Besides being a 'functionary of capital' obedient to the laws of capital, he may possess a distinct personality and may regard this fact as a decisive factor in the production process. The value of a commodity – profit – is *realized* in circulation: it may therefore appear as though it arose from it,

an appearance which is especially reinforced by two circumstances: first, the profit made in selling depends on cheating, deceit, inside knowledge, skill and a thousand favourable market opportunities; and then by the circumstance that added here to labour-time is a second determining element – time of circulation.[139]

Marx points out that rates of profit, although they differ between one enterprise and another, tend to approximate to an *average profit*, which individual capitalists are always trying to transcend by competitive struggle. 'In fact, the direct interest taken by the capitalist, or the capital, of any individual sphere of production in the exploitation of the labourers who are directly employed is confined to making an extra gain, either through exceptional overwork, or reduction of the wage below the average, or through the exceptional productivity of the labour employed.' But the most important fact is that the *total* capital is based on surplus value – profit – and is therefore interested in the exploitation of the workers, the varying degree of exploitation depending on the length of the working-day and the intensity of work.

A further tendency of the capitalist mode of production is that of the *fall in the rate of profit* simultaneous with the *growth of the mass of profit*. Capital invested in the instruments of labour (i.e. constant capital) grows with increasing production, whereas the ratio of variable to constant capital decreases.

The drive of capital towards ever-increasing production, constant expansion of value and accumulation, the change in the relative proportions of constant and variable capital, the need for increasing exploitation as well as increasing consumption, the development of the productive power of labour so that more things are produced with the same capital and the same amount of work, and, lastly, the fall in the rate of profit all give rise to contradictory tendencies and phenomena until at last the profound contradiction inherent in capitalism can no longer be disguised.

Alongside the fall in the rate of profit the mass of capital grows, and hand in hand with this there occurs a depreciation of existing capitals which checks the fall and gives an accelerating motion to the accumulation of capital-values.

Alongside the development of productivity there develops a higher composition of capital, i.e. the relative decrease of the ratio of variable to constant capital.

These different influences may at one time operate predominantly side by side in space, and at another succeed each other in time. From time to time the conflict of antagonistic agencies finds vent in crises. The crises are always but momentary and forcible solutions of the existing contradictions. They are violent eruptions which for a time restore the disturbed equilibrium.

The contradiction, to put it in a very general way, consists in that the capitalist mode of production involves a tendency towards absolute development of the productive forces, regardless of the value and surplus-value it contains, and regardless of the social conditions under which capitalist production takes place; while, on the other hand, its aim is to preserve the value limit (i.e. to promote an ever more rapid growth of this value).[140]

The tendency towards unrestrained production and unlimited development of the productive forces enters into contradiction with the maintenance of existing capital value.

Capitalist production seeks continually to overcome these immanent barriers, but overcomes them only by means which again place these barriers in its way and on a more formidable scale.

The *real barrier* of capitalist production is *capital itself*. It is that capital and its self-expansion appear as the starting and the closing point, the motive and the purpose of production; that production is only production for *capital* and not vice versa, the means of production are not mere means for a constant expansion of the living process of the *society* of producers. The limits within which the preservation or self-expansion of the value of capital resting on the expropriation and pauperization of the great mass of producers can alone move – these limits come continually into conflict with the methods of production employed by capital for its purposes, which drive towards unlimited extension of production, towards production as an end in itself, towards unconditional development of the social productivity of labour. The means – unconditional development of the productive forces of society – comes continually into conflict with the limited purpose, the self-expansion of the existing capital.[141]

With accumulation and concentration, capital's inherent tendency towards *over-production* is intensified. This, of course, does not mean over-production of *use-values* – the masses of mankind could do with many more of these – but of *exchange-values*, of commodities which cannot find a buyer.

Since the aim of capital is not to minister to certain wants, but to produce profit, and since it accomplishes this purpose by methods which adapt the mass of production to the scale of production, not *vice versa*, a rift must continually ensue between the limited dimensions of consumption under capitalism and a production which forever tends to exceed this immanent barrier.[142]

There are not too many necessities of life produced, in proportion to the existing population. Quite the reverse. Too little is produced to satisfy decently and humanely the wants of the great mass.

There are not too many means of production produced to employ the able-bodied portion of the population. Quite the reverse. In the first place, too large a portion of the produced population is not really capable of working, and is through force of circumstances made dependent on exploiting the labour of others, or on labour which can pass under this name only under a miserable mode of production. In the second place, not enough means of production are produced to permit the employment of the entire able-bodied population under the most productive conditions, so that their absolute working period could be shortened by the mass and effectiveness of the constant capital employed.

On the other hand, too many means of labour and necessities of life are produced at times to permit of their serving as means for the exploitation of labourers at a certain rate of profit. Too many commodities are produced to permit of a realization and conversion into new capital of the value and surplus-value contained in them under the conditions of distribution and consumption peculiar to capitalist production, i.e. too many to permit of the consummation of this process without constantly recurring explosions.

Not too much wealth is produced. But at times too much wealth is produced in its capitalistic, self-contradictory forms.

The limitations of the capitalist mode of production come to the surface:

(1) In that the development of the productivity of labour creates out of the falling rate of profit a law which at a certain point comes into antagonistic conflict with this development and must be overcome constantly through crises.

(2) In that the expansion or contraction of production are determined by the appropriation of unpaid labour and the proportion of this unpaid labour to materialized labour in general, or, to speak the language of the capitalists, by profit and the proportion of this profit to the employed capital, thus by a definite rate of profit, rather than the relation of production to social requirements, i.e. to the requirements of socially developed human beings . . .

The rate of profit is the motive power of capitalist production. Things are produced only so long as they can be produced with a profit. Hence the concern of the English economists over the decline of the rate of profit. The fact that the bare possibility of this happening should worry Ricardo, shows his profound understanding of the conditions of capitalist production. It is that which is held against him, it is his unconcern about 'human beings', and his having an eye solely for the development of the productive forces, whatever the cost in human beings and capital-*values* – it is precisely that which is the most important thing about him. Development of the productive forces of social labour is the historical task and justification of capital. This is just the way in which it unconsciously creates the material requirements of a higher mode of production.[143]

This passage is doubly significant; it not only shows that Marx preferred the 'cynicism' of bourgeois scientific economists to any sentimental obfuscation of real conditions, but also proves his historical objectivity. Marx was ruthless in unmasking the dehumanizing effects of capitalism; he passionately championed the working class and strove to develop its political consciousness; and yet he was also an objective historian who, while attacking a system, never overlooked its 'historical task and justification'. He described the origins of capital and its 'primitive accumulation' with all its cruelties, but he also paid tribute to the historic role of capital. The chapter entitled 'The So-Called Primitive Accumulation'[144] is one of the most magnificent and exciting passages in written history, and its content justifies the almost Shakespearean sentence: 'If money, according to Augier,* "comes into the world with a congenital blood-stain on one cheek", capital comes dripping from head to foot, from every pore, with blood and dirt.'[145]

Just as Marx saw *alienation* as the sombre shadow cast upon the earth by the *division of labour*, whilst being able to affirm the division of labour as a stage in the development by which man progresses towards his full potential of humanity, so too he called for the struggle against capitalism in order to accelerate the transition – represented by capitalism – to higher social forms.

Surplus-labour in general, as labour performed over and above the given requirement, must always remain. . . . It is one of the civilizing aspects of capital that it enforces this surplus-labour in a manner and under conditions which are more advantageous to

* Emile Augier (1820–89), French dramatist and author, a harsh critic of the social conditions of his time. – *Author's note.*

the development of the productive forces, social relations, and the creation of the elements for a new and higher form than under the preceding forms of slavery, serfdom, etc. Thus it gives rise to a stage, on the one hand, in which coercion and monopolization of a social development (including its material and intellectual advantages) by one portion of society at the expense of the other are eliminated; on the other hand, it creates the material means and embryonic conditions, making it possible in a higher form of society to combine this surplus-labour with a greater reduction of time devoted to material labour in general.[146]

'The great historical aspect of capital,' Marx wrote in the draft *Foundations of the Critique of Political Economy*,

is that it *creates surplus labour*. . . . Capital as a ceaseless striving after the universal form of wealth drives labour beyond the confines of natural necessity and so creates the material element for the development of a rich individuality, which is as many-sided in its production as it is in its consumption. Thus the labour of this individuality will no longer appear as labour but as the full development of action itself, from which natural necessity in its immediate form has disappeared; because natural necessity has been replaced by historically created necessity. Therefore *capital is productive*, i.e. it is an essential relationship for the development of the social productive forces. It only ceases to be such where the development of these productive forces finds itself limited by capital.[147]

In every economic crisis the productive forces find themselves limited by capital. But the bourgeoisie has learnt some lessons: it cannot break down the barrier, but it can push it farther back; it cannot avoid crises, but it can mitigate them. The unexampled growth of productive forces in our time has confronted the bourgeoisie with new problems, but it has also enriched it with new opportunities.

Marx assumed that *economic* crises would become increasingly acute, and in his time the assumption was well-founded.

Despite the world economic crisis of 1929, history does not seem to have fulfilled his prediction. But the inner contradictions of the capitalist mode of production, which he analysed, are today plainly to be seen by everyone, including non-Marxists; and *political* crises are indeed becoming more and more catastrophic.

9

THE PROBLEM OF INCREASING MISERY

For the young Marx the increasing misery of the worker was the inevitable result of his alienation. The product of the worker's labour confronts him as an alien, imperious commodity. Owning no means of production, he is thrust into the machinery of production by the stranger who owns them. He labours, not in order to satisfy a need, but because in the world of commodity production there is nothing else left for him to do. Therefore his misery increases, regardless of how high his wages are, in proportion with the volume and importance of his labour. The more wealth he produces, the poorer he becomes, whether his own wage rises or falls in the process. Higher wages do not confer human dignity upon the worker.

Marx, the author of *Capital*, was to remain faithful to this view. In Volume III of *Capital* (Chapter 5), Marx, now an old man, retraced the idea first outlined in the *Economic and Political Manuscripts*. Between the two, it is true, lies the theory of value and surplus value, which placed the doctrine of increasing misery upon the foundations of a new political economy.

The production of surplus value is the chief object of capitalist production. Capital always seeks to extract more from the bone, nerve and brain of working-people, be it through the lengthening of the working-day, through intensification of work, or through increased productivity which has the effect of shortening that part of the working-day during which the worker produces a value corresponding to his wage and lengthening that part during which he performs unpaid labour for the capitalist. The capitalist must try, on pain of extinction, to increase productivity in order to resist competition. He must try to lower production costs in order temporarily to undercut his competitors. For this reason the capitalist has to accumulate part of the surplus value, add it to the existing capital, invest it in new machinery, etc. All methods of increasing surplus value are therefore methods of accumulation, and all methods of accumulation are methods of increasing surplus value.

But all methods for the production of surplus-value are at the same time methods of accumulation; and every extension of accumulation becomes again a means for the development of these methods. It follows therefore that in proportion as capital accumulates, the lot of the labourer, be his payment high or low, must grow worse.[148]

The higher wages which workers can win by organized struggle, especially in periods of high employment (i.e. of minimum unemployment), only mean that the weight and strength of the golden chain is such that its tension can be slackened a little.

The worker's miserable condition lies first and foremost in the fact that by his labour he reproduces capital for the benefit of capital, and with it his own alienation and misery.

Capital, which is extremely economical with goods and machines, is recklessly extravagant with living men, with the flesh and blood, the nerve and brain of working-people; nothing is allowed to stand in the way of capital accumulation and increased profit.

Hence Capital is reckless of the health or length of life of the labourer, unless under compulsion from society. To the outcry as to the physical and mental degradation, the premature death, the torture of over-work, it answers: Ought these to trouble us since they increase our profits? But looking at things as a whole, all this does not, indeed, depend on the good or ill will of the individual capitalist. Free competition brings out the inherent laws of capitalist production, in the shape of external coercive laws having power over every individual capitalist.[149]

This ruthless chase after profit, the motive force of capitalist production, creates a continuous tendency towards the increasing misery of the workers; hence 'the general tendency of capitalist production is not to raise, but to sink the average standard of wages' (*Wages, Price and Profit*). The tendency is 'modified' and restrained primarily by the workers themselves, who, especially in periods of high employment, are able to fight it and by doing so can 'make the best of the occasional chances for their temporary improvement'. But the tendency towards the increasing misery of the working class finds continuous expression in the lowering of the workers' relative share in the national income. This share, which is a share in the values produced by the workers themselves, diminishes constantly even in periods of rising wages, while the share of the capitalists increases, so that the workers, even with a rising income, can actually buy a constantly decreasing proportion of the products they have made.

Marx drew attention to several important factors in assessing the position of the working class, which must be taken into account when considering the question of the tendency towards increasing misery. These factors are threefold:

First and foremost there are economic crises, periodically recurrent in Marx's time, which largely cancel out any improvements in the standard of living of the workers and during which their increasing misery becomes patently evident in a number of ways, such as food and housing conditions, and, above all, mass unemployment.

Second, the effects of the intensification of labour, which is a form of lengthening of the working-day. In one hour of 'concentrated' work more can be got out of the worker than in two 'porous' hours; the worker can be forced to expend more than twice as much vital energy. Intensification of work means that the worker's living time is transformed to a still greater degree into labour time for the employer. As a result the worker is liable to age more quickly and becomes unable at an earlier age to keep pace with the working rhythms.

Lastly, the value of labour power (the means of subsistence necessary for the maintenance of the worker and his family) can increasingly be earned only by means of women and children working as well as the head of the family; his wage is no longer sufficient to ensure the maintenance and reproduction of the family and has to be supplemented and replaced by the family wage, the increase in the family income being always less than the increase in the total labour performed.

The value of labour-power was determined, not only by the labour-time necessary to maintain the individual adult labourer, but also by that necessary to maintain his family. Machinery, by throwing every member of that family on to the labour-market, spreads the value of the man's labour-power over his whole family. It thus depreciates his labour-power. To purchase the labour-power of a family of four workers may, perhaps, cost more than it formerly did to purchase the labour-power of the head of the family, but, in return, four days' labour takes the place of one, and their price falls in proportion to the excess of the surplus-labour of four over the surplus-labour of one. In order that the family may live, four people must now, not only labour, but expend surplus-labour for the capitalist. Thus we see that machinery, while augmenting the human material that forms the principal object of capital's exploiting power, at the same time raises the degree of exploitation.[150]

Marx's investigation into the value of *labour power as a commodity* throws an important light on the concrete circumstances in which the capitalist tendency towards increasing misery of the working class is expressed. This value is determined by the value of the means of consumption which are necessary for the production, development and maintenance of a worker's labour power and the maintenance and reproduction of his family. As Marx points out in *Wages, Price and Profit*, this value is made up of two elements: a physical one, determined by the means of consumption necessary for the maintenance and reproduction of labour power and representing the minimum limit of the value, and a historical and social one, the magnitude of which is determined by the class struggle and which is conditioned, in every country, by its particular standard of living and its traditions. In this respect wages take on the colouring of each particular civilization.

The specific social conditions under which men live and work give rise to specific needs whose satisfaction demands consumer goods beyond the minimum limit of the value of labour power. This historical and social element, which is capable of an infinite range of variations and is conditioned by the state of the productive forces, is decided by the class struggle.

The fixation of its actual degree is only settled by the continuous struggle between capital and labour, the capitalist constantly tending to reduce wages to their physical minimum, and to extend the working day to its physical maximum, while the working man constantly presses in the opposite direction. The matter resolves itself into a question of the respective powers of the combatant.[151]

Here we encounter two factors which, in the sense that Marx used the term, 'modify' the tendency towards increasing misery. Progressive technological development and increasing productivity lower the value of labour power by lowering the value of the goods required for its maintenance and reproduction. At the same time they alter social wants and create an automatic necessity to produce new consumer goods. Thus technical progress lowers the value of labour power on the one hand and, on the other hand, creates new demands and new goods as a natural part of that value. The position of the workers must always be measured by the value of labour power, which comprises, *inter alia*, this historical and social element of new demands created by production itself.

A house may be large or small; as long as the surrounding houses are equally small it satisfies all social demands for a dwelling. But let a palace arise beside the little house, and it shrinks from a little house to a hut. The little house shows now that its owner has only very slight or no demands to make; and however high it may shoot up in the course of civilization, if the neighbouring palace grows to an equal or even greater extent, the occupant of the relatively small house will feel more and more uncomfortable, dissatisfied and cramped within its four walls.

A noticeable increase in wages presupposes a rapid growth of productive capital. The rapid growth of productive capital brings about an equally rapid growth of wealth, luxury, social wants, social enjoyments. Thus, although the enjoyments of the worker have risen, the social satisfaction that they give has fallen in comparison with the increased enjoyments of the capitalist, which are inaccessible to the worker, in comparison with the state of development of society in general. Our desires and pleasures spring from society; we measure them, therefore, by society and not by the objects which serve for their satisfaction. Because they are of a social nature, they are of a relative nature.[152]

The second decisive counter-tendency to production for production's sake and the consequent deterioration of the condition of the workers was, Marx thought, the battle fought by the workers themselves. Marx attached great importance to the struggle of the trade unions. At the same time, he believed that what he called the 'general law of capitalist accumulation' set certain fixed limits upon the workers' struggle for improved conditions of life.

The composition of capital changes with accumulation. The portion spent on machinery, construction, raw materials, etc., rises compared with that spent on wages. The latter may increase absolutely, but it is bound to diminish compared with the other part of capital. Hence a part of the labour force is always made redundant by capital accumulation. A relative surplus-population is created – the so-called 'industrial reserve army', displaced by machines and technology – which, especially in periods of crisis, separates out a 'lazarus-layer' of the most wretched paupers, and which constantly depresses the wage level of the employed.

This is the absolute general law of capitalist accumulation. Like all other laws it is modified in its working by many circumstances . . .[153]

It establishes an accumulation of misery corresponding with accumulation of capital. Accumulation of wealth at one pole is, therefore, at the same time accumulation of misery, agony of toil, slavery, ignorance, brutality, mental degradation at the opposite pole, i.e. on the side of the class that produces its own product in the form of capital.[154]

The antagonistic character of capitalist production, that is to say the irreconcilable class antagonism between capital and labour, finds its clearest and most brutal expression in times of economic crises. But the law applies to all periods of capitalist production and depresses the situation of the worker, 'be his payment high or low', at all times.

Unlike his critics and some of his disciples, Marx never actually used the concept of a 'theory of increasing misery'. But the general law of capitalist accumulation does represent a theory of increasing misery, since it is obvious that Marx did not regard the workers' struggle as an adequate counter-tendency to the continuous formation of industrial reserve armies and the simultaneous de-classing of layers of the proletariat. In this respect Marx has been proved wrong, at least so far as the workers in the advanced capitalist countries are concerned. But in the global sense his broad historical vision proved correct when he pointed out that in assessing the situation of workers it was necessary to consider the world market as a whole, and that the wages of some could rise only because others were starving.

10

THE THEORY OF REVOLUTION

The theory of revolution is the consequence and the concentrated expression of Marx's view of historical development, that is to say of the sequence of social formations in history. In their struggle for a living, in their dialogue with nature, men develop certain instruments, tools, forms of labour, and experiences which Marx described as productive forces; and he described as production relations the relations governing men's existence, which are essentially dependent on who owns the means of production. He saw the driving force of social development in the historical tendency towards establishing production relations (or property relations) which correspond to the level of development and the character of the productive forces at any time. In this 'law of motion of history' – always activated by social groups, classes whose interests coincide with the developing tendency – he saw the key to understanding the sequence of the various forms of social order (primitive communism, slavery, feudalism, capitalism), though not quite according to the simple linear scheme later to be drawn in various textbooks of Marxism. On the evidence of the transition from feudalism to capitalism, of bourgeois revolutions, one might say of Western European history in general, he methodically and concretely modified the law of historical motion, and with it the theory of socialist revolution. Nevertheless, in the already quoted *Preface to a Contribution to the*

Critique of Political Economy he expanded the particular to the general.

In the social production of their life, men enter into definite relations that are indispensable and independent of their will, relations of production which correspond to a definite stage of development of their material productive forces. . . . At a certain stage of their development the material productive forces of society come in conflict with the existing relations of production, or – what is but a legal expression for the same thing – with the property relations within which they have been at work hitherto. From forms of development of the productive forces these relations turn into their fetters. Then begins an epoch of social revolution.[155]

Wherein did Marx see the conflict between productive forces and production relations which leads to socialist revolution?

The development of productive forces under capitalism extends their social character, and this finds expression in the creation of major enterprises, the increasing co-ordination of labour processes, the intermingling of production processes and the dominant role of industrial production in society as a whole. Capitalist ownership of the means of production and capitalist appropriation of the product become, at a certain point, fetters on the development of the productive forces; this is particularly evident in the periodically recurring crises which, Marx assumed both in the *Communist Manifesto* and in *Capital*, would become continually more violent and all-embracing. In these 'epidemics of overproduction' the social character of production revolts against capitalist property relations. The social character of production demands social ownership of the means of production.

Economic crises bring this conflict into the open. 'The ultimate reason for all real crises always remains the poverty and restricted consumption of the masses as opposed to the drive of capitalist production to develop the productive forces as though only the absolute consuming power of society constituted their limit.'[156]

Let us recall once more the passage in *Capital* which we have already quoted:

The monopoly of capital becomes a fetter upon the mode of production, which has sprung up and flourished along with, and under it. Centralization of the means of production and socialization of labour at last reach a point where they become incompatible with their capitalist integument. This integument is burst asunder. The knell of capitalist private property sounds. The expropriators are expropriated.[157]

The *Communist Manifesto*, twenty years earlier, had already drawn the comparison with the bourgeois revolution:

At a certain stage in the development of these means of production and of exchange, the conditions under which feudal society produced and exchanged, the feudal organization of agriculture and manufacturing industry, in one word, the feudal relations of property became no longer compatible with the already developed productive forces; they became so many fetters. They had to be burst asunder; they were burst asunder.

Into their place stepped free competition, accompanied by a social and political constitution adapted to it, and by the economic and political sway of the bourgeois class.

A similar movement is going on before our own eyes. Modern bourgeois society with its relations of production, of exchange and of property, a society that has conjured up such gigantic means of production and of exchange, is like the sorcerer, who is no longer able to control the powers of the nether world whom he has called up by his spells. For many a decade past the history of industry and commerce is but the history of the revolt of modern productive forces against modern conditions of production, against the property relations that are the conditions for the existence of the bourgeoisie and of its rule.[158]

But the transition to socialism does not take place automatically. It is enforced by the revolution of the working class, for this class, itself 'the greatest productive force', suffers more than any other from the conflict between productive forces and production relations. Since under capitalism there is production only as long as there is profit, the socialization of the means of production is the special interest of the working class. It has only 'to set free the elements of the new society with which old collapsing bourgeois society itself is pregnant'.[159]

The notion that the social character of the productive forces is already pressing for recognition within capitalist society and seeking to establish forms of property and production compatible with itself is an important one which has often been overlooked in later exposés of Marxist doctrine. At first Marx believed that stock companies were an expression of the incompatibility between the volume of the means of production and private property:

The capital, which in itself rests on a social mode of production and presupposes a social concentration of means of production and labour-power, is here directly endowed with the form of social capital (capital of directly associated individuals) as distinct from private capital, and its undertakings assume the form of social undertakings as distinct from private undertakings. It is the abolition of capital as private property within the framework of capitalist production itself.[160]

This result of the ultimate development of capitalist production is a necessary transitional phase towards the reconversion of capital into the property of producers, although no longer as the private property of the individual producers, but rather as the property of associated producers, as outright social property. On the other hand, the stock company is a transition towards the conversion of all functions in the reproduction process which still remain linked with capitalist property, into mere functions of associated producers, into social functions.[161]

Marx regarded this process, which later led to the formation of monopolies and trusts and culminated in forms of state ownership, as being related to a partial recognition by the capitalists of the social character of the productive forces. He saw the process as evidence that the capitalist had forfeited his function, a fact also confirmed by the increasing separation between ownership and administrative control – the administration of enterprises being taken over more and more by 'managers' (Marx already employed this term). In a historical sense the capitalist owner had lost his function, and the working class, again in a historical sense, had the task of openly appropriating the means of production on behalf of society and, by socializing the means of production, assisting the increasingly evident social character of production to assert itself.

This being so, it is natural that Marx should have expected the social revolution to occur more or less simultaneously in the developed countries of Western Europe, and most probably first in the most industrially developed country – England. Superb diagnostician though Marx was, history failed to confirm this prognosis. The means of production were first socialized in backward countries – a historical fact which accounts for the central problems of Marxism and the labour movement today. Yet it is interesting and significant from the viewpoint of the later development of Marxism and the labour movement that backward countries can temporarily move into the forefront of revolutionary development and that the unresolved problems of the bourgeois revolution can act as detonators for a transition to the socialist revolution. Already in the *Communist Manifesto* we read the following highly significant passage:

The Communists turn their attention chiefly to Germany, because that country is on the eve of a bourgeois revolution that is bound to be carried out under more advanced conditions of European civilization, and with a much more developed proletariat, than that of England was in the seventeenth, and of France in the eighteenth century, and because the bourgeois revolution in Germany will be but the prelude to an immediately following proletarian revolution.[162]

This doubtless represented a certain revision of the 'law of motion'. To put it crudely, it meant that the backwardness of a country could prove beneficial to revolutionary perspectives, the unused reserves of the bourgeois revolution acting as fuel for the socialist revolution. Marx persisted in this view after the collapse of the revolution of 1848 in Germany, but with the subtle difference that he allotted to the petty-bourgeois democrats the role of leaders of a bourgeois revolution. This revolution would content itself with social reforms, and it was the task of the working class to develop it into a socialist revolution reaching beyond the frontiers of Germany. In the *Address of the Central Committee to the Communist League* of March 1850 we read:

While the democratic petty bourgeois wish to bring the revolution to a conclusion as quickly as possible, and with the achievement, at most, of the above demands, it is our interest and our task to make the revolution permanent, until all more or less possessing classes have been forced out of their position of dominance, until the proletariat has conquered state power, and the association of proletarians, not only in one country but in all the dominant countries of the world, has advanced so far that competition among the proletarians of these countries has ceased and that at least the decisive productive forces are concentrated in the hands of the proletarians . . .
If the German workers are not able to attain power and achieve their own class interests without completely going through a lengthy revolutionary development, they at least know for a certainty this time that the first act of this approaching revolu-

tionary drama will coincide with the direct victory of their own class in France and will be very much accelerated by it . . .

Their battle cry must be: The Revolution in Permanence.[163]

This document later gained great importance in the argument on 'permanent revolution' within the Bolshevik party, an argument that was to have extremely grave consequences. But even in the 1880s Marx was already 'turning his attention chiefly' to Russia, because there, 'with a much more developed proletariat than that of England in the seventeenth and France in the eighteenth century' – and in some respects than that of Germany of the 1840s – the bourgeois revolution was the order of the day. The preface to the Russian edition of the *Communist Manifesto* in 1882 named Russia as 'the vanguard of revolutionary action in Europe' and even spoke of the possibility that the Russian village community might pass directly to communist common ownership. But Russia, the backward country – like Germany forty years previously – was allotted the role of initial detonator destined to touch off a socialist revolution, whose actual arena would be in developed Western Europe:

If the Russian Revolution becomes the signal for a proletarian revolution in the West, so that both complement each other, the present Russian common ownership of land may serve as the starting point for a communist development.[164]

Marx saw the essential content of the socialist revolution in the transfer of the means of production into public ownership, a process which was to take place under the leadership of the working class as having a greater interest in it than any other class. The question of the form in which this process was to occur – by peaceful or violent means – was for Marx a secondary issue, and his attitude towards it differed considerably at different times. Generally speaking, the older Marx remained faithful to the young Marx's view that violence is *midwife* to every society pregnant with a new one: but he never maintained that violence *begets* the new society. Thus it was not a fundamental inconsistency when he wrote in *The Poverty of Philosophy*, the *Communist Manifesto* and other works that the rule of the proletariat could be founded only on the forcible overthrow of the bourgeoisie, or, in a letter to his friend Kugelmann in 1871, that it was essential for every real people's revolution on the continent to 'smash' the machinery of the State – while at the same time speaking of the possibility of a peaceful revolution in America, England and Holland. He oriented the members of the International towards both possibilities:

We must declare to the governments: we know that you are the armed power which is directed against the proletariat; we shall proceed against you by peaceful means where possible, and by force of arms if necessary.[165]

II

DICTATORSHIP OF THE PROLETARIAT, SOCIALISM, COMMUNISM

Going beyond Hegel's conception of the State, the young Marx analysed the State as a political expression of human alienation, an instrument, created by men, which had made itself independent and was turned against its creators. Marx always remained faithful to this interpretation, viewing the state apparatus as a product alienated from the society which produced it. This apparatus, Marx believed, serves the ruling classes, but also acquires a certain independence, especially in situations where the classes are in temporary equilibrium. Its tendency towards autonomy grows stronger in such situations and results in phenomena such as Bonapartism, when a dictator supported by the state apparatus can appoint himself the guardian of the nation. Marx believed that one of the principal tasks of the socialist revolution was to overcome this political alienation, this alienated political power.

'The working class,' Marx wrote in *The Poverty of Philosophy*,

in the course of its development, will substitute for the old civil society an association which will exclude classes and their antagonism, and there will be no more political power properly so-called, since political power is precisely the official expression of antagonism in civil society.[166]

In *The Poverty of Philosophy* civil war appears as a

pre-condition of this goal, as it does in the *Communist Manifesto* a year later, where Marx's ideas concerning the forms of revolution and the tasks of the victorious proletariat are stated more precisely:

In depicting the most general phases of the development of the proletariat we traced the more or less veiled civil war, raging within existing society, up to the point where that war breaks out into open revolution, and where the violent overthrow of the bourgeoisie lays the foundation for the sway of the proletariat . . .

We have seen above that the first step in the revolution by the working class is to raise the proletariat to the position of ruling class, to win the battle of democracy.

The proletariat will use its political supremacy to wrest, by degrees, all capital from the bourgeoisie, to centralize all instruments of production in the hands of the State, i.e. of the proletariat organized as the ruling class; and to increase the total of productive forces as rapidly as possible.[167]

With this idea, too, Marx kept faith all his life. The elevation of the proletariat to the position of a ruling class, the establishment of a state under the leadership of the working class – for which French socialists of the period employed the term 'dictatorship of the proletariat' – means the achievement of democracy, the creation of conditions which render it possible to transfer the means of production into public ownership. The state which comes into being as a result of violent struggle against the exploiting classes is a state under the leadership of the victorious proletariat, the majority of the people, and in that sense, therefore, a democratic state. The *Manifesto* makes no mention of the complete abolition of state power, but this vision remains inherent in Marx's concept of the state.

We have already said that Marx modified the law of motion of history and with it the socialist revolution, principally of the transition from feudalism to capitalism, that is to say of Western European history. The theory of the socialist revolution was largely influenced by the experience of the three French Revolutions of 1789, 1830 and 1848. The concept of the State was largely conditioned by the analysis of the French state, on the basis of the experience of the Revolution of 1848 and the *coup d'état* of Napoleon III. It seemed more than ever necessary to Marx to smash the rigidly organized state apparatus in order to leave the way free for a development that would lead via the rule of the proletariat to the abolition of all state power; and this seemed possible only in the aftermath of a civil war. Marx retained this conviction, so far as France was concerned, even at a time when he allowed for the possibility of a peaceful development in England, America and Holland, where the state apparatus had not at that time attained the centralized power it had in France. We should recall that eight years after Marx's death Engels regarded this possibility as conceivable for France too.

However, in *The Eighteenth Brumaire of Louis Bonaparte* the statement is unequivocal:

But the revolution is thoroughgoing. It is still journeying through purgatory. It does its work methodically. By 2 December 1851 it had completed one half of its preparatory work; it is now completing the other half. First it perfected the parliamentary power, in order to be able to overthrow it. Now that it has attained this, it perfects the *executive power*, reduces it to its purest expression, isolates it, sets it up against itself as the sole target, in order to concentrate all its forces of destruction against it. And when it has done this second half of its preliminary work, Europe will leap from its seat and exultantly exclaim: Well grubbed, old mole!

This executive power with its enormous bureaucratic and military organization, with its ingenious state machinery, embracing wide strata, with a host of officials numbering half a million, besides an army of another half million, this appalling parasitic body, which enmeshes the body of French society like a net and chokes all its pores, sprang up in the days of the absolute monarchy, with the decay of the feudal system, which it helped to hasten. . . . The first French Revolution . . . developed . . . centralization, but at the same time the extent, the attributes and the agents of governmental power. Napoleon perfected this state machinery. The Legitimist monarchy and the July monarchy added nothing but a greater division of labour. . . . Finally . . . the parliamentary republic found itself compelled to strengthen, along with the repressive measures, the resources and centralization of governmental power. All revolutions perfected this machine instead of smashing it. The parties that contended in turn for domination regarded the possession of this huge state edifice as the principal spoils of the victor.[168]

For the state to be created after the smashing of the centralist, parasitic state apparatus, a state led by the working class and gradually socializing the means of production, Marx took over the concept of the 'dictatorship of the proletariat'. Within this concept was implicit the vision of grand and violent struggles and victories, but also of increasing democracy for the masses of the population. Marx wrote to his friend Josef Weydemeyer on 5 March 1852:

And now as to myself, no credit is due to me for discovering the existence of classes in modern society, nor yet the struggle between them. Long before me bourgeois historians had described the historical development of this struggle of the classes and bourgeois economists the economic anatomy of the classes. What I did that was new was to prove: (1) that the *existence of classes* is only bound up with *particular historical phases in the development of production*; (2) that the class struggle necessarily leads to the *dictatorship of the proletariat*; (3) that this dictatorship itself only constitutes the transition to the *abolition of all classes* and to a *classless society*.[169]

Marx's concept of the state, then, was modified in the light of the events in France from 1848 to 1852. His view of a new state under the leadership of the working class – the state of the socialist revolution, and the functions of such a state – was modified and made concrete by the example of the Paris Commune of 1871. He regarded the short-lived Paris Commune as the first form of a workers' government, which by its practical actions and the measures it adopted had proved that the transition to socialism is bound up with a fundamentally new state system. Such a state system is no longer a state in the old sense of the word, because, after the smashing of the old state apparatus, it develops forms of popular control over the executive and the bureaucracy which correspond to the vision of the abolition of all central political power. We read in *The Civil War in France*, which appeared directly after the defeat of the Paris Commune, that the nineteenth century saw the development of 'centralized State power, with its ubiquitous organs of standing army, police, bureaucracy, clergy, and judicature' – a power whose origins went back to the Middle Ages. With the intensification of class antagonism between capital and labour

the State power assumed more and more the character of the national power of capital over labour, of a public force organized for social enslavement, of an engine of class despotism. After every revolution marking a progressive phase in the class struggle, the purely repressive character of the State power stands out in bolder and bolder relief.

After the revolution of 1848 State power became 'the national war-engine of capital against labour'. The Second Empire reinforced this state of affairs.

'The direct antithesis of the empire was the Commune.' The Commune was the distinct form of 'a Republic that was not to supersede the monarchical form of class-rule, but class-rule itself'.

'The first decree of the Commune . . . was the suppression

of the standing army, and the substitution for it of the armed people.'

The Commune was formed of the municipal councillors, chosen by universal suffrage in the various wards of the town, responsible and revocable at short terms. The majority of its members were naturally working men, or acknowledged representatives of the working class. . . . Instead of continuing to be the agent of the Central Government, the police was at once stripped of its political attributes, and turned into the responsible and at all times revocable agent of the Commune. So were the officials of all other branches of the Administration. From the members of the Commune downwards the public service had to be done at *workmen's wages*. The vested interests and the representation allowances of the high dignitaries of State disappeared along with the high dignitaries themselves. . . . The judicial functionaries were to be divested of that sham independence which had but served to mask their abject subservience to all succeeding governments . . . magistrates and judges were to be elective, responsible, and revocable.

Eight years after Marx's death Frederick Engels described these fundamental features of the new state form in an introduction to the third edition of *The Civil War in France*, as follows:

It was precisely the oppressing power of the former centralized government, army, political police, bureaucracy, which Napoleon had created and which since then had been taken over by every new government as a welcome instrument and used against its opponents – it was precisely this power which was to fall everywhere, just as it had already fallen in Paris.

From the very outset the Commune was compelled to recognize that the working class, once come to power, could not go on managing with the old state machine; that in order not to lose again its only just conquered supremacy, this working class must, on the one hand, do away with all the old repressive machinery previously used against it itself, and, on the other, safeguard itself against its own deputies and officials, by declaring them all, without exception, subject to recall at any moment ...

Against this transformation of the state and the organs of the state from servants of society into masters of society – an inevitable transformation in all previous states – the Commune made use of two infallible means. In the first place, it filled all posts – administrative, judicial and educational – by election on the basis of universal suffrage of all concerned, subject to the right of recall at any time by the same electors. And, in the second place, all officials, high or low, were paid only the wages received by other workers. The highest salary paid by the Commune to anyone was 6,000 francs. In this way an effective barrier to place-hunting and careerism was set up, even apart from the binding mandates to delegates to representative bodies which were added besides ...

The Commune was to be a working, not a parliamentary, body, executive and legislative at the same time ...

Instead of deciding once in three or six years which member of the ruling class was to misrepresent the people in Parliament, universal suffrage was to serve the people, constituted in Communes, as individual suffrage serves every other employer in the search for the workmen and managers in his business.[170]

Control from below, democracy spreading from below to the top, the democratic abolition of political alienation as he had described it in his youth – in these features lay the significance of the Paris Commune for Marx. He saw them as vitally important for the socialist states to come, for future dictatorships of the proletariat operating 'as the transition to the abolition of classes and with them of the state'.[171]

'In a rough sketch of national self-government which the Commune had no time to develop, it states clearly that the Commune was to be the political form of even the smallest country hamlet.' The Communes, too, were to elect deputies to the National Delegation in Paris:

The few but important functions which still would remain for a central government were not to be suppressed, as has been intentionally mis-stated, but were to be discharged by Communal, and therefore strictly responsible agents. The unity of the nation was not to be broken, but, on the contrary, to be organized by the Communal Constitution, and to become a reality by the destruction of the State power which claimed to be the embodiment of that unity independent of, and superior to, the nation itself, from which it was but a parasitic excrescence. While the merely repressive organs of the old governmental power were to be amputated, its legitimate functions were to be wrested from an authority usurping pre-eminence over society itself, and restored to the responsible agents of society.

The Communal Constitution would have restored to the social body all the forces hitherto absorbed by the State parasite feeding upon, and clogging the free movement of, society. By this one act it would have initiated the regeneration of France . . .

In reality, the Communal Constitution brought the rural producers under the intellectual lead of the central towns of their districts, and there secured to them, in the working men, the natural trustees of their interests. The very existence of the Commune involved, as a matter of course, local municipal liberty, but no longer as a check upon the, now superseded, State power . . .

The multiplicity of interpretations to which the Commune has been subjected, and multiplicity of interests which construed it in their favour, show that it was a thoroughly expansive political form, while all previous forms of government had been emphatically repressive. Its true secret was this. It was essentially a working-class government, the product of the struggle of the producing against the appropriating class, the political form at last discovered under which to work out the economic emancipation of labour.

Except on this last condition, the Communal Constitution would have been an impossibility and a delusion.[172]

It is within this meaning of a 'dictatorship of the proletariat' that we should understand Marx's celebrated dictum in the *Critique of the Gotha Programme*, written four years after the Paris Commune:

Between capitalist and communist society lies the period of the revolutionary transformation of the one into the other. There corresponds to this also a political transition period in which the state can be nothing but the *revolutionary dictatorship of the proletariat*.[173]

In this work Marx distinguishes two phases in the development of communist society, the first or lower phase when it is still 'stamped with the birthmarks of the old society from whose womb it emerges' and when it distributes the available consumer goods according to the principle of performance, and the second phase – Communism – in which the sources of production are already flowing so abundantly that to each may be given according to his needs:

With an equal performance of labour and hence an equal share in the social consumption fund, one will in fact receive more than another, one will be richer than another, and so on. To avoid all these defects, right instead of being equal would have to be unequal.

But these defects are inevitable in the first phase of communist society as it is when it has just emerged after prolonged birth pangs from capitalist society. Right can never be higher than the economic structure of society and its cultural development conditioned thereby.

In a higher phase of communist society, after the enslaving subordination of the individual to the division of labour, and therewith also the antithesis between mental and physical labour, has vanished; after the productive forces have also increased with the all-round development of the individual, and all the springs of cooperative wealth flow more abundantly – only then can the narrow horizon of bourgeois right be crossed in its entirety and society inscribe on its banners: From each according to his ability, to each according to his needs![174]

From the context of Marx's whole body of ideas it emerges with certainty that he imagined the victory of the revolution and of socialism as a more or less simultaneous process in the advanced capitalist countries, and that the social order he had before his mind's eye was the one of which the *Communist Manifesto* had said: '. . . the free development of each is the condition for the free development of all'.

12

LABOUR MOVEMENT
AND INTERNATIONAL

As part of his theory of revolution and his concept of theory, Marx saw the proletariat as the social force destined, because of its position within the production process and within history, to accomplish the transition to the socialist way of life – not because workers are gods, but because the inhumanity of capitalist society assumes its most concentrated form in the conditions of their life. In *The Holy Family* the young Marx wrote:

The proletariat executes the sentence that private property pronounced on itself by begetting the proletariat, just as it carries out the sentence that wage-labour pronounced on itself by bringing forth wealth for others and misery for itself . . .

When socialist writers ascribe this historic role to the proletariat, it is not, as Critical Criticism pretends to think, because they consider the proletarians as *gods*. Rather the contrary. Since the abstraction of all humanity, even of the *semblance* of humanity, is practically complete in the full-grown proletariat; since the conditions of life of the proletariat sum up all the conditions of life of society today in all their inhuman acuity; since man has lost himself in the proletariat, yet at the same time has not only gained theoretical consciousness of that loss, but through urgent, no longer disguisable, absolutely imperative *need* – that practical expression of *necessity* – is driven directly to revolt against that inhumanity; it follows that the proletariat can and must free itself. But it cannot free itself without abolishing the conditions of its own life. It cannot abolish the conditions of its own life without abolishing *all* the inhuman conditions of life of society today which are summed up in its own situation. Not in vain does it go through the stern but steeling school of *labour*. The question is not what this or that proletarian, or even the whole of the proletariat at the moment *considers* as its aim. The question is *what the proletariat is*, and what, consequent on that *being*, it will be compelled to do. Its aim and historical action is irrevocably and obviously demonstrated in its own life situation as well as in the whole organization of bourgeois society today.[175]

Marx never hesitated to attack narrow craft attitudes within the labour movement and to uphold the necessity for a scientific understanding of social conditions as a basis for political action. Concerning the 'League of the Just' (from which originated the League of Communists on whose behalf Marx and Engels composed the *Communist Manifesto*), he once wrote that 'scientific insight into the economic structure of bourgeois society' had to be established as the 'only tenable theoretical basis', and an explanation in popular form had to be given that 'we are not concerned with imposing some utopian system, but with self-conscious participation in the historical process of revolutionizing society, which is taking place before our eyes'.[176]

Marx emphasized this concept of a realistic, scientifically founded labour policy after the defeat of the revolution of 1848 when, as often happens after the failure of a revolutionary movement, actions and initiatives of all kinds were being proposed within the League of Communists in order to avoid having to face the reality of the situation. At a meeting held on 15 September 1850, when a split in the League occurred, Marx described the opposing attitudes in the following terms:

The minority puts a dogmatic view in place of the critical, and an idealist one in place of the materialist. They regard mere discontent, instead of real conditions, as the driving wheel of revolution. Whereas we tell the workers: You have to go through fifteen, twenty, fifty years of civil wars and national struggles, not only in order to change conditions but also to change yourselves and make yourself capable of political rule; you, on the contrary, say: 'We must come to power immediately, or else we may as well go to sleep.' Whilst we make a special point of directing the German workers' attention to the undeveloped state of the German proletariat, you flatter the national feeling and the status-prejudice of the German artisans in the crudest possible way – which, admittedly, is more popular. Just as the word 'people' has been made holy by the democrats, so the word 'proletariat' has been made holy by you.[177]

For more than a decade Marx regarded his and Engels's writings and scientific studies as the decisive activity on behalf of the Party – the Party not in the narrow but in the historical sense.

Marx re-entered the political labour movement only when 'real forces' were once again in play. At the foundation meeting of the Working Men's International Association (First International) on 28 September 1864, he at first sat in silence on the tribune; later the meeting invited him to compose its 'inaugural address' and in that way he became its intellectual leader. He felt that such direct participation in the movement interfered with his scientific work, once saying bitterly that the International hung upon him 'like an incubus', and he refused to take part in several congresses in order to continue writing *Capital*, whose completion he regarded as extremely important for the movement as well as from other points of view. Yet in the *Inaugural Address*, in numerous documents, statements and lectures, and finally in the *Address on the Civil War in France*, he developed the concept of an international labour movement based on a scientific insight into social development, the recognition of the existence of different pre-conditions for the struggle in different countries, and international solidarity. Only in 1873, ten years before his death, when the International went into dissolution, did he retire from direct participation in organized activity.

The *Inaugural Address* set the workers the task of capturing political power, but it also emphasized the need to force the State to recognize the workers' demands even before the social revolution. Concerning the English Ten Hours' Bill it states:

This struggle about the legal restriction of the hours of labour raged the more fiercely since, apart from frightened avarice, it told indeed upon the great contest between the blind rule of the supply and demand laws which form the political economy of the middle class, and social production controlled by economic foresight, which forms the political economy of the working class. Hence the Ten Hours' Bill was not only a great practical success; it was the victory of a principle; it was the first time that in broad daylight the political economy of the middle class succumbed to the political economy of the working class.[178]

At the same time the *Address* evaluated the co-operative societies of its time as concrete proof of the historical out-datedness of capitalist ownership of the means of production, even if they were by no means as yet capable of breaking the capitalist monopoly:

By deed, instead of by argument, they have shown that production on a large scale, and in accord with the behests of modern science, may be carried on without the existence of a class of masters employing a class of hands; that to bear fruit, the means of labour need not be monopolized as a means of dominion over, and of extortion against, the labouring man himself; and that, like slave labour, like serf labour, hired labour is but a transitory and inferior form, destined to disappear before associated labour plying its toil with a willing hand, a ready mind, and a joyous heart.[179]

Labour movements must also intervene in the foreign

policies of their respective countries, watch the diplomatic acts of their governments, master the mysteries of international politics and vindicate the simple laws of morals and justice, such as ought to govern relations between private individuals, as 'the rules paramount of the intercourse of nations'. Like the *Communist Manifesto*, the *Address* ends with the words: Proletarians of all countries, Unite!

It is not without interest that the International was founded at a demonstration of solidarity with the oppressed Poles; and it was in reference to the Irish question that Marx pronounced his famous dictum that a nation cannot be free so long as it oppresses others.

Within the framework of the International's activities Marx allotted a most important place to trade unions and to socio-political claims. *Wages, Price and Profit*, an address delivered to the General Council of the International, was in essence a detailed reply to the argument that higher wages must inevitably lead to higher prices. The English trade unions* felt Marx's arguments to be of direct help to them. The Geneva Congress of the International in 1866 – a Congress Marx did not attend because of his work on *Capital* – affirmed that labour protection laws do not strengthen the ruling power but modify the relationship of forces in the interest of the workers. The same congress also demanded the eight-hour day and described the trade unions as the means of opposing the numerical strength of the proletariat to the concentrated social power of capital.

The importance of the trade unions was also stressed in a circular letter of the International dealing with the views of

---

*The earliest beginnings of the British trade union movement can be traced back to the period in the eighteenth century which followed the repeal of laws regulating wages and labour conditions. The trade unions were banned between 1799 and 1824; thereafter they developed rapidly. First Trades Union Congress, 1868.

Bakunin* and the sections dominated by his supporters. In this circular Marx wrote‡

The first phase of the struggle of the proletariat against the bourgeoisie is characterized by the movement of sects. This has some justice at a time when the proletariat is not yet sufficiently developed to act as a class. Isolated thinkers undertake the critique of the social contradictions and want to remove them by fanciful solutions which the mass of the workers has only to accept, propagate and put into action. It is in the nature of the sects which form around such pioneers that they alienate themselves from the trade unions and, in a word, from every mass movement. The mass of the proletariat remains indifferent or even hostile towards their propaganda. The workers of Paris and Lyons care as little for the Saint-Simonists,† the Fourierists‡

‡ Michael Bakunin (1814–76), Russian socialist and anarchist, centre of the Russian socialist emigration in central and western Europe, member of the International 1868; expelled 1872; break with Marx 1873. The collective-communist anarchism preached by Bakunin advocated the abolition of the state, religion and marriage; quite generally, he rejected the notion of any power being exercised by men over other men.

† Saint-Simonists: followers of the French social critic Claude-Henri de Rouvroy, Count Saint-Simon (1760–1825). Saint-Simon began by criticizing the economic egoism of the bourgeoisie, wanted to solve the social problem by the moral renewal of mankind, attacked property, and called for the abolition of the law of inheritance and the transfer of the means of production into the ownership of the community. He founded his doctrine on a philosophy of history according to which history shows a constantly increasing tendency towards socialization. Saint-Simon had a great influence on French socialism in the nineteenth century and on the positivism of Auguste Comte.

‡ Fourierists: followers of the French social philosopher Charles Fourier (1772–1837), who outlined a comprehensive system of utopian socialism in the form of a federative association of small autarchic communities (*phalanstères*), which should aim directly at peace and happiness. Fourier's doctrine, whose object was to create integrated production, consumption and living communities, exercised a great influence on the development of trade union organizations.

and the Icarians* as do the English Chartists† and trade
unionists for the Owenites.‡
Originally a lever of the movement, they become an impediment
to it as soon as they are overtaken by it. Then they become
reactionary.[180]

The argument with Bakunin's supporters, who insisted on
mandatory atheism, the abolition of all religious practices,
immediate abolition of the laws of inheritance, etc., and refused
any activity that did not lead directly and immediately to the
triumph of the working class, was directed above all at the
phraseology of sectarianism within the labour movement.
Marx dismissed their programme as a hotch-potch of hack-
neyed commonplaces and thoughtless twaddle, a string of
empty-headed notions aimed merely at a certain momentary

---

* Icarians: followers of the French utopian communist Etienne
Cabet (1788–1856), one of the leading members of the Carbonari
League. In his book *Voyage to Icaria* (1842) Cabet sketched out an
ideal communist society.

† Chartists: the first democratic socialist workers' movement in
England, formed around 1832. Their demands, set forth in the
'People's Charter' of 1838 (universal male suffrage, parliamentary
reform, social legislation) were rejected by Parliament and a rebellion
in Birmingham in 1839 was suppressed. Chartism came to an end
towards 1848 as a result of the growing strength of the English trade
union movement. In its struggle for political equality and social
protection of the workers it had a lasting formative effect on the masses,
whose class consciousness was aroused and encouraged, especially, by
the creation of the first independent workers' press.

‡ Owenites: followers of the English social reformer and socialist,
Robert Owen (1771–1858), who was the first industrialist to introduce
socio-political measures such as shorter working hours, limitation of
child labour, sickness benefits, old age pensions and co-operative
trading. Owen strove in vain for the establishment of a labour exchange
in London and the creation of a labour currency in England. In his
later years he followed markedly utopian tendencies. His experiment
to set up a communist settlement in the United States was a failure.
Owen may be considered the founder of the English trade unions.

effect. As for the immediate abolition of the laws of inheritance, slave ownership was not the result of laws which permitted such ownership, but the other way about. Abolition of the laws of inheritance was no more a starting point for social revolution than abolition of the laws governing contracts between buyers and sellers was possible so long as commodity exchange existed. Marx's sensitivity towards sectarianism is clearly demonstrated in the following letter written to his son-in-law, Paul Lafargue, on 18 April 1870:

Dear Paul-Laurent,
I send enclosed the credentials for M. H. Vernet. Let him give to the new section he is about to establish no *sectarian 'name'*, either Communistic or other. Il faut èviter les *'étiquettes'* sectaires dans l'Association Internationale. The general aspirations and tendencies of the working class emanate from the real conditions in which it finds itself placed. They are therefore common to the whole class although the movement reflects itself in their heads in the most diversified forms, more or less phantastical, more or less adequate. Those to interpret best the hidden sense of the class struggle going on before our eyes – the Communists – are the last to commit the blunder of affecting or fostering Sectarianism.[181]

True, Marx was equally allergic to all the vague phrases of 'too-wise pundits' who wanted to give a 'higher idealistic twist' to socialism, i.e. to replace the materialist basis (which requires serious objective study if one desires to operate upon it) by a modern mythology with its goddesses Liberty, Equality and Fraternity. In the *Critique of the Gotha Programme* Marx was harsh in his dismissal of all vague and muddled formulations.

When the young Marx first met Parisian workers who professed the Communal ideal, he was immensely struck by the nobility that shone in their faces. The *Address of the General Council of the International*, which, under the title of *The Civil*

War in France, describes and comments on the struggles and the end of the Paris Commune, is full of admiration for the militancy and self-sacrifice of the workers of Paris and for their deep sense of solidarity. We have already referred to some theoretical aspects of this work. On 12 April 1872 Marx wrote to his friend Kugelmann:

What elasticity, what historical initiative, what a capacity for sacrifice in these Parisians! After six months of hunger and ruin, caused rather by internal treachery than by the external enemy, they rise, beneath Prussian bayonets, as if there had never been a war between France and Germany and the enemy were not at the gates of Paris. History has no like example of a like greatness . . .
Compare these Parisians, storming heaven, with the slaves to heaven of the German-Prussian Holy Roman Empire, with its posthumous masquerades reeking of the barracks, the Church, cabbage-junkerdom and above all, of the philistine . . .[182]

The Address itself closed with the words:

Working men's Paris, with its Commune, will be for ever celebrated as the glorious harbinger of a new society. Its martyrs are enshrined in the great heart of the working class. Its exterminators history has already nailed to that eternal pillory from which all the prayers of the priests will not avail to redeem them.[183]

It was genuine modesty linked with deep respect for the great struggles and sacrifices of working people which made Marx write concerning certain events within the German social-democratic movement:

'I bear no grudge' (as Heine has it), and neither does Engels. Neither of us gives tuppence for popularity. Example of my dislike for any personality cult: during the time of the International I never allowed the numerous manoeuvres to acclaim me, by which I was plagued from various countries, to penetrate into the sphere of publicity, nor have I ever replied to them, except now and then with a slap.[184]

13

THE PHILOSOPHY
OF PRACTICE

The chief defect of all materialism up to now (including
Feuerbach's) is, that the object, reality, which we apprehend
through our senses, is understood only in the form of the *object*
of *contemplation*; but not as *sensuous human activity*, as *practice*;
not subjectively. Hence in opposition to materialism the *active*
side was developed abstractly by idealism – which of course does
not know real sensuous activity as such.[185]

With these sentences begin the eleven theses on the materialist philosopher Ludwig Feuerbach which Marx entered in his
notebook in 1845 but which, unfortunately, he never developed
to a complete 'philosophy of practice'. 'The brilliant germ of
the new world outlook', as Engels called these notes, did, of
course, ripen in later economic, sociological and political
writings. In this sketch of a new philosophy there beats the
pulse of a life's work. And yet it is a pity that Marx never found
time to combine into a major work what he had noted down
and later in many respects developed.

In the limited space available to us, and which perhaps we
have already filled too densely, a few brief indications must
suffice.

The 'philosophy of practice' is intimately connected with
the vision of the 'whole', 'total' man. From the very start the
species man has not appropriated the world *passively* but
actively, through practice, labour, the setting of goals, the
giving of form. As men *changed* the world they expanded and
refined their ability to *know* it, and the growing capacity for

cognition again enhanced their ability to change it. Man creates himself by his works; by his estrangement from himself he becomes his own creator.

But the process of the division of labour led to a profound split between intellectual and physical work. In the commodity-producing society philosophy ceased to be the business of the *active* man and became that of the *contemplative* man, the man who does not change the world but observes it, reflects upon it, interprets it.

A curious inversion had taken place in the development of philosophy. In *idealist philosophy* the intellectual became the *active*, creative principle; for Fichte, the 'I' (not the individual but the cosmic I) was the world creator; for Hegel, the 'world spirit' works itself through all stages of 'estrangement' to an all-embracing self-consciousness. For the *materialist philosophers*, on the other hand, man was only a *product* of the outside world and that world itself only an *object* for contemplation, reflected in sensory impressions, of which thoughts were regarded as the abstraction.

The 'philosophy of practice' transfers the active, creative principle from the systems of idealist philosophy into materialism: reality as process, movement, change, and *social reality* as the *interaction* of objective and subjective factors, of *objective* circumstances and *human* activity.

Men are thinking beings; but the extent to which 'objective truth is an attribute of human thought', the Second Thesis states,

is not a theoretical but a *practical* question. Man must prove the truth, i.e. the reality and power, the 'this-sidedness' of his thinking in practice. The dispute over the reality or non-reality of thinking that is isolated from practice is a purely *scholastic* question.

Thus truth is an attribute of thought in so far as thought

corresponds to reality; and only practice can prove the extent to which it does so. If a theory fails in practice, that is to say if practice contradicts it not only momentarily but persistently over a long period, the theory must either be rejected or corrected. Faced with a momentary, transient contradiction in practice it may be correct or approximately correct, but it must prove its power and reality by its development. Practice always decides.

Men are *active* beings; they change, so far as they are able, the circumstances they find to their advantage. 'All social life is essentially *practical*', states the Eighth Thesis. 'All the mysteries which urge theory into mysticism find their rational solution in human practice and in the comprehension of this practice.' Human practice alone is not enough; in the 'wood of blindness' a madman can lead men to disaster. It must be *comprehended* practice. To comprehend it is the function of revolutionary philosophy. This philosophy does not proceed from categories, not from general, broad principles, but from men; it examines *what* they do, asks *why* they do it, for what purpose and under what compulsion, it teaches them to *know* what they do, that is to say it learns from practice so as to teach practice to become *self-cognition*.

The philosophy of practice denies both the assumption that man is *autonomous* and can decide independently at any time, and the opposite, i.e. that man only *appears* to decide while in reality circumstances rule men's lives and do not admit of any genuine decision. 'Man' is an abstraction: there are only men, human beings, who have their species-nature – the nature that distinguishes them from all other organisms – in common, but who belong to a particular social formation, a class, a nation, a historical epoch and are therefore *conditioned* by the totality of these circumstances in their mode of behaviour, their possibilities, needs and decisions at any given time.

'The essence of man,' Marx retorts to Feuerbach, 'is no

abstraction inherent in each separate individual. In its reality it is the *ensemble* (aggregate) of social relations.' Feuerbach postulates 'an abstract – *isolated* – human individual' and therefore does not see 'that the abstract individual whom he analyses belongs to a particular form of society'. (Sixth and Seventh Theses.) The *concrete* human being is therefore to be understood not only as ' "genus", the inward, dumb generality which *naturally* unites the many individuals', but also as a *social* being creating itself and realizing its potential in its historical development. The 'aggregate' of social relations which makes up the human being includes not only the momentary social condition but also *that which has become* – e.g. language, custom, tradition – and *that which is in process of becoming*, that which stirs as contradiction in the womb of established society and announces itself as a possibility.

Hence man is not an isolated 'I' and is not capable of abolishing contradictions and re-educating others merely through acts of his consciousness, through 'enlightenment' or 'philosophy'. Philosophy needs practice in order to become effective. This principle is demonstrated in the Fourth Thesis using Feuerbach as an example:

Feuerbach starts out from the fact of religious self-estrange-ment, of the duplication of the world into a religious and a secular one. His work consists in resolving the religious world into its secular basis. But that the secular basis raises itself above itself and establishes for itself an independent realm in the clouds can be explained only through the cleavage and self-contra-dictions within this secular basis. The latter must therefore in itself be both understood in its contradiction and revolutionized in practice.

Marx strongly emphasized the material and social condition-ing of all human thought and action, i.e. he completely rejected 'voluntarism', the notion that the human will is capable of overcoming the limitations of given circumstances. But, equally, he was convinced of the capacity of men to change these given circumstances. 'The materialistic doctrine concerning the changing of circumstances and education forgets that circumstances are changed by men and that the educator himself must be educated.' (Third Thesis.)

It seems to us that this *dynamism* inherent in the philosophy of practice gains special significance in an age when immense, apparently independent power apparatuses and mechanisms set in motion by the rapidly growing productive forces tend to make us feel that man is nothing and that the product is all, and somehow creates independently from human striving, knowledge and action. The 'systems', 'structures', 'orders' are supposed to follow immutable laws of their own, and any attempt to fight this is viewed as romantic, antiquated humanism. The anti-human is considered, as it were, a cosmic law and total surrender to total reification is a consequence of scientific thinking and deep-frozen knowledge. Ours is therefore a time when we can least of all afford to forget that men, though they are formed by circumstances, are at the same time capable of changing circumstances; the great problem always being that the educator himself must be educated, that the changing of circumstances requires changed men (or rather men engaged in changing themselves), that the humanization of society is not a natural process but presupposes human beings with unusual moral and intellectual qualities – human beings capable of transcending given circumstances.

A materialism which merely *contemplates* the world and regards it as the *object* of scientific observation does not go beyond the limits of the given situation, i.e. of bourgeois society. Refusing to criticize or to set itself any aim, it becomes willy-nilly an *affirmation of what exists*. 'The highest point to which contemplative materialism can attain, i.e. that materialism which does not comprehend our sensuous nature as practical activity, is the contemplation of separate individuals and of civil society.' (Ninth Thesis.) When this materialism no longer contemplates the separate individuals but regards them only as statistical units, as representatives of average modes of behaviour, it becomes the philosophy, freed of all humanism, of bourgeois society at a late stage of development. For individual man is more than an invention of individualism.

'The standpoint of the old type of materialism is civil society, the standpoint of the new materialism is human society or social humanity.' (Tenth Thesis.)

The *Theses on Feuerbach* were the foundation for this new materialism beginning and ending with man, a humanist philosophy of practice. If the standpoint of this philosophy is human society or social humanity, it adopts the standpoint of an as yet unattained level of development, a real but as yet unrealized possibility. In it, social tendencies concentrate into aims. In it, the self-cognition of practice becomes one of the essential factors of practice.

Philosophy without practice dissolves very easily into air or smoke or congeals into a dogmatic profession of faith: practice without philosophy turns into myopic, mindless practicism.

The philosophy of practice is a philosophy, i.e. not merely a collection of partial scientific findings from various spheres of study, but an attempt to understand the workings of a *total process*. It is the philosophy of *practice*, i.e. not merely thought drawn from and tested against practice, but also thought that helps practice towards self-cognition and thus contributes to its development.

By observing and interpreting changes as they occur, the philosophy of practice gains cognition which is never at a standstill; by the never-ending endeavour to affect the development of the changing world, it continually transcends pure observation and interpretation and becomes a motive force of practice. The celebrated Eleventh Thesis with which the notes on Feuerbach end is, therefore, not an either/or but a synthesis of philosophical interpretation and of the practical transforming of the world:

'The philosophers have only *interpreted* the world differently, the point is, to *change* it.'

14

MARXISM TODAY

The world of Marx's ideas is not a closed system. Development, amplification, enlargement are intrinsic in it. To treat it in Marx's own spirit is to speak of its history, its past, its present – and of its future, which has already begun.

After Marx's death, around the turn of the century, his ideas permeated the labour movements especially in Germany, Austria and Russia and helped to form the world view of hundreds of thousands of people, acquiring, however, the accent of natural history which turned the desired development towards a socialist society into an 'iron Must of history' and, even after heavy defeats, kept alive the conviction that 'the world is ours despite everything'. Not the least cause of this was the fact that Karl Kautsky, the principal popularizer of Marxism, had a background of Darwinism and, invoking certain passages of Marx, but more especially Engels, imposed on the Marxist view of history a determinism deriving from natural history. The most important critique of this view of history was undoubtedly Lenin's *What Is To Be Done?* (1902).

Proceeding from Marx's reflections, Lenin adapted the theory of revolution to the particular problems of Tsarist Russia. Unused reserves for bourgeois revolution could, Lenin thought, become the fuel for a socialist one, though only – in view of the already advanced level of economic development – under the leadership of the proletariat. The latter had first of all to win over the peasant masses in order to carry through the unsolved tasks of the bourgeois agrarian revolution: then the development would be driven forward to socialist revolution under the leadership of the proletariat. It is true that, even shortly before the October Revolution, Lenin still believed that the revolutionary development in Russia would only play the role of an initial detonator of the socialist revolution which – in accordance with Marx's idea – had to take place in the advanced capitalist countries.

Proceeding from Marx, invoking Marx, Lenin coupled this idea with an analysis of structural changes within capitalism. The latter, he said, had developed from a capitalism of free competition to monopoly capitalism, as Hilferding* in particular had shown. Lenin termed this stage of capitalism – monopoly capitalism – *imperialism*. It meant that the whole world was drawn into the capitalist system; hence the revolutionary perspectives were concentrated on world revolution, which did not necessarily have to begin in an industrially developed country and by no means had to occur simultaneously in the most advanced capitalist countries. Lenin attached decisive importance to the national revolutionary movements in the colonies and semi-colonies.

Leninism was the term applied during Lenin's lifetime to the ideas of that group (the Bolsheviks) of which Lenin had been the leader within Russian social democracy and under whose leadership the October Revolution of 1917 took place. After Lenin's death these views were simplified into a system which Stalin named Marxism-Leninism, or 'Marxism in the era of imperialism and proletarian revolution'. Mao Tse-tung

---

* Rudolf Hilferding (1877–1941). German financial expert and social democrat, originally 'Austro-Marxist', twice German finance minister in periods of crisis, attempting to deal with inflation in 1923 and to re-stabilize Germany's finances without raising taxes or reducing wages. Assassinated by the Nazis.

invoked this system when developing a theory of revolution which linked the problems of agrarian revolution with the national and anti-colonial revolution and which viewed the peasants as the principal force in the revolutionary struggle, although with formal recognition of the leadership of the proletariat.

At the present time we can distinguish four principal variants of Marxist thought which are of effective interest for the future:

(a) Marxism as the world view of scientific thinkers who regard the Marxist theory of history as an application of dialectical materialism to history. This view is founded on the works of Engels rather than of Marx, but has, of late, also taken account of Engels's dictum that materialism must change with every important new discovery. With this in mind, Engels's own ideas are being re-considered, his simplifications are being eliminated, and certain prohibitions, which proclaimed important discoveries of modern science to be un-Marxist, are being removed.

(b) Marxism as the 'philosophy of man', with alienation as the fundamental concept.

(c) Marxism as a hierarchically organized structure of concepts distinguished by the novelty of its sphere of problems and its conceptual network. This is an attempt to apply structuralism, which has opened up valuable new ground in linguistics and in the analysis of myths, to Marxist theory and, by the 'symptomatic' reading of Marx, to discover those nodal points in the structure of concepts of which Marx himself was not conscious.

(d) The interpretation of Marxism as a scientific methodology of the study of history and of political initiative. This variant corresponds to the ideas which we developed in the chapters on *Historical Materialism* and *The Philosophy of*

Practice. It was represented especially by Antonio Gramsci*
who represented an unorthodox trend in the socialist movement
before the First World War and in the communist movement
between the wars. On this basis religious believers, too, are
able to profess Marxism.

The influence of Marx today transcends the boundaries of
Marxism. We find that the modern social sciences – sociology,
political economy, historical theory, etc. – have absorbed many
of the important ideas developed by Marx, so that, as C. Wright
Mills† wrote, these sciences are unimaginable without them
. . . if only as something to contest.

* Antonio Gramsci (1891–1937), intellectual leader of Italian
communism, author of important works of philosophy, sociology,
history and literary criticism, written for the most part in gaol. A
parliamentary deputy, he was imprisoned by Mussolini in 1926 and
died in 1937 after ten years of prison.

† C. Wright Mills (1916–62), leading American sociologist, author
of *White Collar, The Power Élite, The Causes of World War Three,
The Marxists*, etc.

APPENDIX

It would be a pity if all that our readers knew of Marx's writings were derived from a mosaic of brief quotations. In this appendix we reproduce a few longer passages characteristic of Marx as a thinker and stylist.

We have chosen for this purpose the reflections on the philosophy of history which form the opening of *The Eighteenth Brumaire of Louis Bonaparte* (1852), the *Preface to A Contribution to the Critique of Political Economy* (1859), which gives a brief exposé of the principles of historical materialism, and the 'Preface' to the first volume of *Capital* (1867).

Instead of presenting these passages in chronological order, we print first the *Preface* of 1859 because of its biographical interest.

PREFACE TO A CONTRIBUTION TO THE CRITIQUE OF POLITICAL ECONOMY[186]

... I was taking up law, which discipline, however, I only pursued as a subordinate subject along with philosophy and history. In the year 1842–43, as editor of the *Rheinische Zeitung*, I experienced for the first time the embarrassment of having to take part in discussions on so-called material interests. The proceedings of the Rhenish Landtag on thefts of wood and parcelling of landed property, the official polemic which Herr von Schaper, then *Oberpräsident* of the Rhine Province, opened against the *Rheinische Zeitung* on the conditions of the Moselle peasantry, and finally debates on free trade and protective tariffs provided the first occasions for occupying myself with economic questions. On the other hand, at that time when the good will to 'go farther' greatly outweighed knowledge of the subject, a philosophically weakly tinged echo of French Socialism and Communism made itself audible in the *Rheinische Zeitung*. I declared myself against this amateurism, but frankly confessed at the same time in a controversy with the *Allgemeine Augsburger Zeitung* that my previous studies did not permit me even to venture any judgment on the content of the French tendencies. Instead, I eagerly seized on the illusion of the managers of the *Rheinische Zeitung*, who thought that by a weaker attitude on the part of the paper they could secure a remission of the death sentence passed upon it, to withdraw from the public stage into the study.

The first work which I undertook for a solution of the doubts which assailed me was a critical review of the Hegelian philosophy of right, a work the introduction to which appeared in 1844 in the *Deutsch-Französische Jahrbücher*, published in Paris. My investigation led to the result that legal relations as well as forms of state are to be grasped neither from themselves nor from the so-called general development of the human mind, but rather have their roots in the material conditions of life, the sum total of which Hegel, following the example of the Englishmen and Frenchmen of the eighteenth century, combines under the name of 'civil society', that however the anatomy of civil society is to be sought in political economy. The investigation of the latter, which I began in Paris, I continued in Brussels, whither I had emigrated in consequence of an expulsion order of M. Guizot. The general result at which I arrived and which, once won, served as a guiding thread for my studies, can be briefly formulated as follows: In the social production of their life, men enter into definite relations that are indispensable and independent of their will, relations of production which correspond to a definite stage of development of their material productive forces. The sum total of these relations of production constitutes the economic structure of society, the real foundation, on which rises a legal and political superstructure and to which correspond definite forms of social consciousness. The mode of production of material life conditions the social, political and intellectual life process in general. It is not the consciousness of men that determines their being, but, on the contrary, their social being that determines their consciousness. At a certain stage of their development, the material productive forces of society come in conflict with the existing relations of production, or – what is but a legal expression for the same thing – with the property relations within which they have been at work hitherto. From forms of development of the productive forces these relations turn into their fetters. Then begins an epoch of social revolution. With the change of the economic foundation the entire immense superstructure is more or less rapidly transformed. In considering such transformations a distinction should always be made between the material transformation of the economic conditions of production, which can be determined with the precision of natural science, and the legal, political, religious, esthetic or philosophic – in short, ideological forms in which men become conscious of this conflict and fight it out. Just as our opinion of an individual is not based on what he thinks of himself, so can we not judge of such a period of transformation by its own consciousness; on the contrary, this consciousness must be explained rather from the contradictions of material life, from the existing conflict between the social productive forces and the relations of production. No social order ever perishes before all the productive forces for which there is room in it have developed; and new, higher relations of production never appear before the material conditions of their existence have matured in the womb of the old society itself. Therefore mankind always sets itself only such tasks as it can solve; since, looking at the matter more closely, it will always be found that the task itself arises only when the material conditions for its solution already exist or are at least in the process of formation. In broad outline Asiatic, ancient, feudal, and modern bourgeois modes of production can be designated as progressive epochs in the economic formation of society. The bourgeois relations of production are the last antagonistic form of the social process of production – antagonistic not in the sense of individual antagonism, but of one arising from the social conditions of life of the individuals; at the same time the productive forces developing in the womb of bourgeois society create the material conditions for the solution of that antagonism. This social formation brings, therefore, the pre-history of human society to a close.

Frederick Engels, with whom, since the appearance of his brilliant sketch on the criticism of the economic categories (in the *Deutsch-Französische Jahrbücher*), I had maintained a constant exchange of ideas by correspondence, had by another road (compare his *The Condition of the Working Class in England in 1844*) arrived at the same result as I, and when in the spring of 1845 he also settled in Brussels, we resolved to work out in common the opposition of our view to the ideological view of German philosophy, in fact, to settle accounts with our erstwhile philosophical conscience. The resolve was carried out, in the form of a criticism of post-Hegelian philosophy. The manuscript, two large octavo volumes, had long reached its place of publication in Westphalia when we received the news that altered circumstances did not allow of its being printed. We abandoned the manuscript to the gnawing criticism of the mice all the more willingly as we had achieved our main purpose – self-clarification. Of the scattered works in which we put our views before the public at that time, now from one aspect, now from another, I will mention only the *Manifesto of the Communist Party*, jointly written by Engels and myself, and *Discours sur le libre échange*, published by me. The decisive points of our view were first scientifically, although only polemically, indicated in my work published in 1847 and directed against Proudhon: *Misère de la philosophie*, etc. A dissertation written in German on *Wage Labour*, in which I put together my lectures on this subject delivered in the Brussels German Workers' Society, was interrupted, while being printed, by the February Revolution and my consequent forcible removal from Belgium.

The editing of the *Neue Rheinische Zeitung* in 1848 and 1849, and the subsequent events, interrupted my economic studies which could only be resumed in the year 1850 in London. The enormous material for the history of political economy which is accumulated in the British Museum, the favourable vantage point afforded by London for the observation of bourgeois society, and finally the new stage of development upon which the latter appeared to have entered with the discovery of gold in California and Australia, determined me to begin afresh from the very beginning and to work through the new material critically. These studies led partly of themselves into apparently quite remote subjects on which I had to dwell for a shorter or longer period. Especially, however, was the time at my disposal curtailed by the imperative necessity of earning my living. My contributions, during eight years now, to the first English-American newspaper, the *New York Tribune*, compelled an extraordinary scattering of my studies, since I occupy myself with newspaper correspondence proper only in exceptional cases. However, articles on striking economic events in England and on the Continent constituted so considerable a part of my contributions that I was compelled to make myself familiar with practical details which lie outside the sphere of the actual science of political economy.

This sketch of the course of my studies in the sphere of political economy is intended only to show that my views, however they may be judged and however little they may coincide with the interested prejudices of the ruling classes, are the result of conscientious investigation lasting many years. But at the entrance to science, as at the entrance to hell, the demand must be posted:

> *Qui si convien lasciare ogni sospetto;*
> *Ogni viltà convien che qui sia morta.*

London, January 1859   KARL MARX

THE EIGHTEENTH BRUMAIRE OF LOUIS BONAPARTE[187]

Hegel remarks somewhere that all facts and personages of great importance in world history occur, as it were, twice. He forgot to add: the first time as tragedy, the second as farce. Caussidière for Danton, Louis Blanc for Robespierre, the *Montagne* of 1848 to 1851 for the *Montagne* of 1793 to 1795, the Nephew for the Uncle. And the same caricature occurs in the circumstances attending the second edition of the eighteenth Brumaire!

Men make their own history, but they do not make it just as they please; they do not make it under circumstances chosen by themselves, but under circumstances directly encountered, given and transmitted from the past. The tradition of all the dead generations weighs like a nightmare on the brain of the living. And just when they seem engaged in revolutionizing themselves and things, in creating something that has never yet existed, precisely in such periods of revolutionary crisis they anxiously conjure up the spirits of the past to their service and borrow from them names, battle cries and costumes in order to present the new scene of world history in this time-honoured disguise and this borrowed language. Thus Luther donned the mask of the Apostle Paul, the Revolution of 1789 to 1814 draped itself alternately as the Roman republic and the Roman empire, and the Revolution of 1848 knew nothing better to do than to parody, now 1789, now the revolutionary tradition of 1793 to 1795. In like manner a beginner who has learnt a new language always translates it back into his mother tongue, but he has assimilated the spirit of the new language and can produce freely in it only when he finds his way in it without recalling the old and forgets his native tongue in the use of the new.

Consideration of this conjuring up of the dead of world history reveals at once a salient difference. Camille Desmoulins, Danton, Robespierre, Saint-Just, Napoleon, the heroes as well as the parties and the masses of the old French Revolution, performed the task of their time in Roman costume and with Roman phrases, the task of unchaining and setting up modern *bourgeois* society. The first ones knocked the feudal basis to pieces and mowed off the feudal heads which had grown on it. The other created inside France the conditions under which alone free competition could be developed, parcelled landed property exploited and the unchained industrial productive

power of the nation employed; and beyond the French borders
he everywhere swept the feudal institutions away, so far as was
necessary to furnish bourgeois society in France with a suitable
up-to-date environment on the European Continent. The new
social formation once established, the antediluvian Colossi
disappeared and with them disappeared Romanity – the
Brutuses, Gracchi, Publicolas, the tribunes, the senators, and
Caesar himself. Bourgeois society in its sober reality had begotten
its true interpreters and mouthpieces in the Says, Cousins,
Royer-Collards, Benjamin Constants and Guizots; its real
military leaders sat behind the office desks, and the hog-headed
Louis XVIII was its political chief. Wholly absorbed in the
production of wealth and in peaceful competitive struggle, it no
longer comprehended that ghosts from the days of Rome had
watched over its cradle. But unheroic as bourgeois society is, it
nevertheless took heroism, sacrifice, terror, civil war and battles
of peoples to bring it into being. And in the classically austere
traditions of the Roman republic its gladiators found the ideals
and the art forms, the self-deceptions that they needed in order
to conceal from themselves the bourgeois limitations of the
content of their struggles and to keep their enthusiasm on the
high plane of the great historical tragedy. Similarly, at another
stage of development, a century earlier, Cromwell and the
English people had borrowed speech, passions and illusions from
the Old Testament for their bourgeois revolution. When the real
aim had been achieved, when the bourgeois transformation of
English society had been accomplished, Locke supplanted
Habakkuk.

Thus the awakening of the dead in those revolutions served
the purpose of glorifying the new struggles, not of parodying the
old; of magnifying the given task in imagination, not of fleeing
from its solution in reality; of finding once more the spirit of
revolution, not of making its ghost walk about again.

From 1848 to 1851 only the ghost of the old revolution walked
about, from Marrast, the *républicain en gants jaunes,** who

* Republican in yellow gloves. – *Ed.*

disguised himself as the old Bailly, down to the adventurer, who hides his commonplace repulsive features under the iron death mask of Napoleon. An entire people, which had imagined that by means of a revolution it had imparted to itself an accelerated power of motion, suddenly finds itself set back into a defunct epoch and, in order that no doubt as to the relapse may be possible, the old data arise again, the old chronology, the old names, the old edicts, which had long become a subject of antiquarian erudition, and the old minions of the law, who had seemed long decayed. The nation feels like that mad Englishman in Bedlam who fancies that he lives in the times of the ancient Pharaohs and daily bemoans the hard labour that he must perform in the Ethiopian mines as a gold digger, immured in this subterranean prison, a dimly burning light fastened to his head, the overseer of the slaves behind him with a long whip, and at the exits a confused welter of barbarian mercenaries, who understand neither the forced labourers in the mines nor one another, since they speak no common language. 'And all this is expected of me', sighs the mad Englishman, 'of me, a freeborn Briton, in order to make gold for the old Pharaohs.' 'In order to pay the debts of the Bonaparte family', sighs the French nation. The Englishman, so long as he was in his right mind, could not get rid of the fixed idea of making gold. The French, so long as they were engaged in revolution, could not get rid of the memory of Napoleon, as the election of 10 December proved. They hankered to return from the perils of revolution to the fleshpots of Egypt, and 2 December 1851 was the answer. They have not only a caricature of the old Napoleon, they have the old Napoleon himself, caricatured as he must appear in the middle of the nineteenth century.

The social revolution of the nineteenth century cannot draw its poetry from the past, but only from the future. It cannot begin with itself before it has stripped off all superstition in regard to the past. Earlier revolutions required recollections of past world history in order to drug themselves concerning their own content. In order to arrive at its own content, the revolution of the nineteenth century must let the dead bury their dead.

There the phrase went beyond the content; here the content goes beyond the phrase.

The February Revolution was a surprise attack, a *taking* of the old society *unawares*, and the people proclaimed this unhoped-for *stroke* as a deed of world importance, ushering in a new epoch. On 2 December the February Revolution is conjured away by a cardsharper's trick, and what seems overthrown is no longer the monarchy but the liberal concessions that were wrung from it by centuries of struggle. Instead of *society* having conquered a new content for itself, it seems that the *state* only returned to its oldest form, to the shamelessly simple domination of the sabre and the cowl. This is the answer to the *coup de main** of February 1848, given by the *coup de tête* of December 1851. Easy come, easy go. Meanwhile the interval of time has not passed by unused. During the years 1848 to 1851 French society has made up, and that by an abbreviated because revolutionary method, for the studies and experiences which, in a regular, so to speak, textbook course of development would have had to precede the February Revolution, if it was to be more than a ruffling of the surface. Society now seems to have fallen back behind its point of departure; it has in truth first to create for itself the revolutionary point of departure, the situation, the relations, the conditions under which alone modern revolution becomes serious.

Bourgeois revolutions, like those of the eighteenth century, storm swiftly from success to success; their dramatic effects outdo each other; men and things seem set in sparkling brilliants; ecstasy is the everyday spirit; but they are short-lived; soon they have attained their zenith, and a long crapulent depression lays hold of society before it learns soberly to assimilate the results of its storm-and-stress period. On the other hand, proletarian revolutions, like those of the nineteenth century, criticize themselves constantly, interrupt themselves continually in their own course, come back to the apparently accomplished in order to begin it afresh, deride with unmerciful thoroughness the

* *Coup de main*: surprise attack. *Coup de tête*: rash act. – *Ed.*

inadequacies, weaknesses and paltrinesses of their first attempts, seem to throw down their adversary only in order that he may draw new strength from the earth and rise again, more gigantic, before them, recoil ever and anon from the indefinite prodigiousness of their own aims, until a situation has been created which makes all turning back impossible, and the conditions themselves cry out:

> *Hic Rhodus, hic salta!**
> *Here is the rose, here dance!*

CAPITAL

A Critical Analysis of Capitalist Production   Volume I

Preface to the First German Edition[188]

The work, the first volume of which I now submit to the public, forms the continuation of my *Zur Kritik der Politischen Ökonomie* (*A Contribution to the Criticism of Political Economy*), published in 1859. The long pause between the first part and the continuation is due to an illness of many years' duration that again and again interrupted my work.

The substance of that earlier work is summarized in the first three chapters of this volume. This is done merely for the sake of connexion and completeness. The presentation of the subject-matter is improved. As far as circumstances in any way permit, many points only hinted at in the earlier book are here worked out more fully, whilst, conversely, points worked out fully there are only touched upon in this volume. The sections on the history of the theories of value and of money are now, of course, left out altogether. The reader of the earlier work will find, however, in the notes to the first chapter additional sources of reference relative to the history of those theories.

* Here is Rhodes, leap here! – This phrase is taken from one of Aesop's fables: A swaggerer claimed to have witnesses to prove that he had once made a remarkable leap at Rhodes, to which he received in reply: 'Why cite witnesses if it is true? Here is Rhodes. Leap here!' In other words: Show right here by action what you can do! – *Ed.*

Every beginning is difficult, holds in all sciences. To understand the first chapter, especially the section that contains the analysis of commodities, will, therefore, present the greatest difficulty. That which concerns more especially the analysis of the substance of value and the magnitude of value, I have, to much as it was possible, popularized. The value-form, whose fully developed shape is the money-form, is very elementary and simple. Nevertheless, the human mind has for more than 2,000 years sought in vain to get to the bottom of it, whilst on the other hand, to the successful analysis of much more composite and complex forms, there has been at least an approximation. Why? Because the body, as an organic whole, is more easy of study than are the cells of that body. In the analysis of economic forms, moreover, neither microscopes nor chemical reagents are of use. The force of abstraction must replace both. But in bourgeois society the commodity-form of the product of labour – or the value-form of the commodity – is the economic cell-form. To the superficial observer the analysis of these forms seems to turn upon minutiae. It does in fact deal with minutiae, but they are of the same order as those dealt with in microscopic anatomy.

With the exception of the section on value-form, therefore, this volume cannot stand accused on the score of difficulty. I presuppose, of course, a reader who is willing to learn something new and therefore to think for himself.

The physicist either observes physical phenomena where they occur in their most typical form and most free from disturbing influence, or, wherever possible, he makes experiments under conditions that assure the occurrence of the phenomenon in its normality. In this work I have to examine the capitalist mode of production, and the conditions of production and exchange corresponding to that mode. Up to the present time their classic ground is England. That is the reason why England is used as the chief illustration in the development of my theoretical ideas. If, however, the German reader shrugs his shoulders at the condition of the English industrial and agricultural labourers, or in optimist fashion comforts himself with the thought that in

Germany things are not nearly so bad; I must plainly tell him, '*De te fabula narratur!*'

Intrinsically it is not a question of the higher or lower degree of development of the social antagonisms that result from the natural laws of capitalist production. It is a question of these laws themselves, of these tendencies working with iron necessity towards inevitable results. The country that is more developed industrially only shows, to the less developed, the image of its own future.

But apart from this. Where capitalist production is fully naturalized among the Germans (for instance, in the factories proper) the condition of things is much worse than in England, because the counterpose of the Factory Acts is wanting. In all other spheres we, like all the rest of Continental Western Europe, suffer not only from the development of capitalist production, but also from the incompleteness of that development. Alongside of modern evils, a whole series of inherited evils oppress us, arising from the passive survival of antiquated modes of production, with their inevitable train of social and political anachronisms. We suffer not only from the living, but from the dead. *Le mort saisit le vif!*

The social statistics of Germany and the rest of Continental Western Europe are, in comparison with those of England, wretchedly compiled. But they raise the veil just enough to let us catch a glimpse of the Medusa head behind it. We should be appalled at the state of things at home, if, as in England, our governments and parliaments appointed periodically commissions of inquiry into economic conditions; if these commissions were armed with the same plenary powers to get at the truth; if it was possible to find for this purpose men as competent, as free from partisanship and respect of persons as are the English factory-inspectors, her medical reporters on public health, her commissioners of inquiry into the exploitation of women and children, into housing and food. Perseus wore a magic cap that the monsters he hunted down might not see him. We draw the magic cap down over eyes and ears as a make-believe that there are no monsters.

Let us not deceive ourselves on this. As in the eighteenth century, the American war of independence sounded the tocsin for the European middle-class, so in the nineteenth century, the American Civil War sounded it for the European working-class. In England the progress of social disintegration is palpable. When it has reached a certain point, it must react on the Continent. There it will take a form more brutal or more humane, according to the development of the working-class itself. Apart from higher motives, therefore, their own most important interests dictate to the classes that are for the nonce the ruling ones, the removal of all legally removable hindrances to the free development of the working-class. For this reason, as well as others, I have given so large a space in this volume to the history, the details, and the results of English factory legislation. One nation can and should learn from others. And even when a society has got upon the right track for the discovery of the natural laws of its movement – and it is the ultimate aim of this work, to lay bare the economic law of motion of modern society – it can neither clear by bold leaps, nor remove by legal enactments, the obstacles offered by the successive phases of its normal development. But it can shorten and lessen the birth-pangs.

To prevent possible misunderstanding, a word. I paint the capitalist and the landlord in no sense *couleur de rose*. But here individuals are dealt with only in so far as they are the personifications of economic categories, embodiments of particular class-relations and class-interests. My standpoint, from which the evolution of the economic formation of society is viewed as a process of natural history, can less than any other make the individual responsible for relations whose creature he socially remains, however much he may subjectively raise himself above them.

In the domain of Political Economy, free scientific inquiry meets not merely the same enemies as in all other domains. The peculiar nature of the material it deals with, summons as foes into the field of battle the most violent, mean and malignant passions of the human breast, the Furies of private interest. The English Established Church, e.g., will more readily pardon an attack on thirty-eight of its thirty-nine articles than on $\frac{1}{39}$ of its income. Nowadays atheism itself is *culpa levis*, as compared with criticism of existing property relations. Nevertheless, there is an unmistakable advance. I refer, e.g., to the Blue book published within the last few weeks: *Correspondence with Her Majesty's Missions Abroad, Regarding Industrial Questions and Trades Unions*. The representatives of the English Crown in foreign countries there declare in so many words that in Germany, in France, to be brief, in all the civilized states of the European Continent, a radical change in the existing relations between capital and labour is as evident and inevitable as in England. At the same time, on the other side of the Atlantic Ocean, Mr Wade, vice-president of the United States, declared in public meetings that, after the abolition of slavery, a radical change of the relations of capital and of property in land is next upon the order of the day. These are signs of the times, not to be hidden by purple mantles or black cassocks. They do not signify that tomorrow a miracle will happen. They show that, within the ruling-classes themselves, a foreboding is dawning, that the present society is no solid crystal, but an organism capable of change, and is constantly changing.

The second volume of this work will treat of the process of the circulation of capital (Book II), and of the varied forms assumed by capital in the course of its development (Book III), the third and last volume (Book IV), the history of the theory.

Every opinion based on scientific criticism I welcome. As to the prejudices of so-called public opinion, to which I have never made concessions, now as aforetime the maxim of the great Florentine is mine:

'*Segui il tuo corse, e lascia dir le genti.*'*

London, 25 July 1867   KARL MARX

* 'Go thy way, and let people talk.' (Dante, *The Divine Comedy*.) – Trans.

NOTES

1. *On the Jewish Question*, in: *Karl Marx: Early Writings*, translated and edited by T. B. Bottomore, London, C. A. Watts, 1963, pp. 24–5.
2. ibid., p. 26.
3. *Marx-Engels Gesamt-Ausgabe* (MEGA), Vol. 1, Berlin, 1932, pp. 99 f.*
4. *Contribution to the Critique of Hegel's Philosophy of Right*, in: Bottomore, *Karl Marx: Early Writings*, p. 45.
5. *Economic and Philosophical Manuscripts*, in: Bottomore, *Karl Marx: Early Writings*, p. 124.
6. ibid., p. 126.
7. *Contribution to the Critique of Hegel's Philosophy of Right*, loc. cit., pp. 43–4.
8. *Economic and Political Manuscripts*, loc. cit., p. 167.
9. *Marx-Engels Werke*, Berlin, 1956, Vol. 1, p. 231.*
10. *The German Ideology*, edited by R. Pascal, International Publishers, New York, 1947, pp. 74–5.
11. *Economic and Political Manuscripts*, loc. cit., p. 157.
12. ibid., pp. 157–8.
13. ibid., p. 158.
14. ibid., p. 159.
15. ibid., p. 153.
16. ibid., p. 154.

* Translations of the entries marked with an asterisk have been supplied by the translator; all others have been taken from published works, as indicated.

17. Letter to Mrs Marx dated 21 June 1856, in: Emile Bottigelli: *Lettres et documents de Karl Marx 1856–1883*, Feltrinelli, Milan, 1958.*

18. *Economic and Political Manuscripts*, loc. cit., pp. 159–60.

19. ibid., p. 162.

20. ibid., p. 162.

21. ibid., p. 155.

22. ibid., p. 176.

23. *Grundrisse der Kritik der Politischen Ökonomie*, Moscow, 1939, p. 539.*

24. *Capital III*, Foreign Languages Publishing House, Moscow, 1959, published in Great Britain by Lawrence & Wishart, pp. 799–800.

25. *Economic and Political Manuscripts*, loc. cit., p. 202.

26. ibid., pp. 213–14.

27. ibid., pp. 127–8.

28. *Capital I*, Foreign Languages Publishing House, Moscow, 1959, published in Great Britain by Lawrence & Wishart, pp. 177–8.

29. *Grundrisse der Kritik der Politischen Ökonomie*, p. 505.*

30. *Capital I*, pp. 179–80.

31. ibid., p. 183.

32. ibid., pp. 183–4.

33. ibid., p. 351.

34. ibid., p. 351.

35. *Grundrisse*, p. 390.*

36. *Capital I*, pp. 351–2.

37. *The German Ideology*, pp. 43–4.

38. *Capital I*, p. 363.

39. *The German Ideology*, pp. 46–7.

40. *Capital I*, p. 403.

41. ibid., p. 420.

42. ibid., pp. 422–4.

43. ibid., pp. 486–8.

44. *The German Ideology*, pp. 65–6.

45. ibid., pp. 22–4.

46. *Grundrisse*, p. 76.*

47. *Economic and Political Manuscripts*, loc. cit., p. 114.
48. ibid., p. 134.
49. MEGA, Vol. 3, pp. 535–6.*
50. ibid., p. 536.*
51. ibid., p. 536.*
52. ibid., pp. 539–40.*
53. *Economic and Political Manuscripts*, loc. cit., p. 125.
54. ibid., p. 129.
55. *Grundrisse*, pp. 715 f.*
56. *Economic and Political Manuscripts*, loc. cit., p. 138.
57. ibid., p. 121.
58. *Capital I*, pp. 35–6.
59. ibid., pp. 37–8.
60. ibid., p. 71.
61. ibid., pp. 72–3.
62. ibid., p. 77.
63. *Grundrisse*, p. 75.*
64. *Capital I*, pp. 84–5.
65. *Economic and Political Manuscripts*, loc. cit., p. 193.
66. ibid., pp. 193–4.
67. *Manifesto of the Communist Party*, Progress Publishers, Moscow, 1952, p. 40.
68. ibid., p. 41.
69. *The German Ideology*, pp. 48–9.
70. *Manifesto of the Communist Party*, pp. 43–4.
71. *The Poverty of Philosophy*, Foreign Languages Publishing House, Moscow, published in Great Britain by Lawrence & Wishart, p. 137.
72. *Capital I*, pp. 718 f.
73. *Manifesto of the Communist Party*, pp. 53–60.
74. *Capital III*, pp. 862–3.
75. *The Eighteenth Brumaire of Louis Bonaparte*, in: *Karl Marx and Frederick Engels: Selected Works in Two Volumes*, Foreign Languages Publishing House, Moscow, 1950, Vol. I, p. 249.
76. ibid., p. 252.
77. ibid., pp. 305–6.

78. ibid., pp. 302–3.
79. *The German Ideology*, p. 39.
80. ibid., p. 40.
81. *Manifesto of the Communist Party*, pp. 56–7.
82. *The German Ideology*, p. 41.
83. *Manifesto of the Communist Party*, pp. 45–6.
84. ibid., p. 58.
85. *Capital I*, p. 763.
86. ibid., p. 763.
87. *Preface to A Contribution to The Critique of Political Economy*, in: Karl Marx and Frederick Engels: *Selected Works in Two Volumes*, Vol. I, pp. 328–9.
88. *Manifesto of the Communist Party*, p. 60.
89. *Capital I*, p. 763.
90. *The Poverty of Philosophy*, p. 122.
91. ibid., p. 196.
92. *Wage Labour and Capital*, in: *Selected Works in Two Volumes*, Vol. I, p. 83.
93. *Contribution to the Critique of Hegel's Philosophy of Right*, loc. cit., p. 52.
94. *Grundrisse*, p. 111.*
95. *The Future Results of British Rule in India*, in: *Selected Works in Two Volumes*, Vol. I, p. 324.
96. *Capital I*, pp. 18–19.
97. *The Holy Family*, Foreign Languages Publishing House, Moscow, 1956, p. 52.
98. ibid., p. 125.
99. *Letter to Bolte dated 23 November 1871*, in: *Selected Works in Two Volumes*, Vol. II, pp. 423–4.
100. *Capital III*, p. 159.
101. *Letters to Dr Kugelmann*, London, Martin Lawrence, p. 125.
102. *The Eighteenth Brumaire of Louis Bonaparte*, loc. cit., p. 229.
103. ibid., p. 263.
104. ibid., p. 225.
105. *The German Ideology*, pp. 28–9.
106. ibid., pp. 197–8.

107. *The Eighteenth Brumaire of Louis Bonaparte*, loc. cit., p. 225.
108. *Capital I*, pp. 59–60.
109. ibid., p. 39.
110. ibid., pp. 39–40.
111. ibid., p. 44.
112. ibid., p. 197.
113. ibid., p. 69.
114. ibid., p. 86.
115. ibid., pp. 101–2.
116. ibid., p. 119.
117. ibid., p. 122.
118. ibid., p. 146.
119. ibid., pp. 151–2.
120. ibid., pp. 152–3.
121. ibid., p. 167.
122. ibid., pp. 168–9.
123. ibid., pp. 170–1.
124. ibid., p. 173.
125. ibid., pp. 193–4.
126. ibid., p. 204.
127. ibid., p. 205.
128. ibid., p. 209.
129. ibid., p. 217.
130. ibid., p. 232.
131. ibid., p. 233.
132. ibid., pp. 234–5.
133. *Capital III*, p. 37.
134. ibid., p. 39.
135. ibid., pp. 42–3.
136. ibid., pp. 47–8.
137. ibid., p. 50.
138. ibid., p. 191.
139. ibid., p. 807.
140. ibid., p. 244.
141. ibid., p. 245.
142. ibid., p. 251.
143. ibid., pp. 252–4.

144. *Capital I*, p. 713.
145. ibid., p. 760.
146. *Capital III*, p. 799.
147. *Grundrisse*, p. 231.*
148. *Capital I*, p. 645.
149. ibid., p. 270.
150. ibid., p. 395.
151. *Wages, Price and Profit*, in: *Selected Works in Two Volumes*, Vol. I, pp. 401–2.
152. *Wage Labour and Capital*, in: *Selected Works in Two Volumes*, Vol. I, p. 87.
153. *Capital I*, p. 644.
154. ibid., p. 645.
155. *Preface to a Contribution to the Critique of Political Economy*, loc. cit., pp. 328–9.
156. *Capital III*, pp. 472–3.
157. *Capital I*, p. 763.
158. *Manifesto of the Communist Party*, pp. 48–9.
159. *The Civil War in France*, in: *Selected Works in Two Volumes*, Vol. I, p. 474.
160. *Capital III*, p. 427.
161. ibid., p. 428.
162. *Manifesto of the Communist Party*, pp. 95–6.
163. *Address of the Central Committee to the Communist League*, in: *Selected Works in Two Volumes*, Vol. I, pp. 102, 108.
164. *Manifesto of the Communist Party*, p. 12.
165. *Marx-Engels Werke*, Berlin, 1956, Vol. 17, p. 652.*
166. *The Poverty of Philosophy*, p. 197.
167. *Manifesto of the Communist Party*, pp. 59, 74.
168. *The Eighteenth Brumaire of Louis Bonaparte*, loc. cit., p. 301.
169. *Letter to Josef Weydemeyer dated 5 March 1852*, in: *Selected Works in Two Volumes*, Vol. II, p. 410.
170. *The Civil War in France*, loc. cit., pp. 471–2.
171. F. Engels, *The Housing Question*, in: *Selected Works in Two Volumes*, Vol. I, p. 555.
172. *The Civil War in France*, loc. cit., pp. 471–4.

73. *Critique of the Gotha Programme*, in: *Selected Works in Two Volumes*, Vol. II, p. 30.

74. ibid., pp. 22–3.

75. *The Holy Family*, pp. 52–3.

76. *Herr Vogt*, Berlin 1953, p. 75.*

77. *Marx-Engels Werke*, Vol. 8, p. 412.*

78. *Inaugural Address of the Working Men's International Association* in: *Selected Works in Two Volumes*, Vol. I, p. 347.

79. ibid., p. 347.

80. *Ein Komplott gegen die Internationale Arbeiterassoziation*, Brunswick, 1874, p. 22.*

81. *Letter to P. Lafargue*, in: Emile Bottigelli: *Lettres et documents de Karl Marx 1856–1883*, Feltrinelli, Milan, 1958, p. 171.

82. *Letters to Dr Kugelmann*, pp. 123–4.

83. *The Civil War in France*, loc. cit., p. 491.

84. Marx/Engels, *Briefe an A. Bebel und andere*, Berlin, 1953, p. 170.*

85. *Theses on Feuerbach*, in: *The German Ideology*, pp. 197–9.

86. *Preface to A Contribution to The Critique of Political Economy*, loc. cit., pp. 327–31.

87. *The Eighteenth Brumaire of Louis Bonaparte*, loc. cit., pp 225–8.

88. *Capital I, Preface to the First German Edition*, pp. 7–11.

INDEX

Index

More about Penguins and Pelicans

Penguinews, which appears every month, contains details of all the new books issued by Penguins as they are published. From time to time it is supplemented by *Penguins in Print*, which is a complete list of all available books published by Penguins. (There are well over four thousand of these.)

A specimen copy of *Penguinews* will be sent to you free on request. For a year's issues (including the complete lists) please send 30p if you live in the United Kingdom, or 60p if you live elsewhere. Just write to Dept EP, Penguin Books Ltd, Harmondsworth, Middlesex, enclosing a cheque or postal order, and your name will be added to the mailing list.

Note: *Penguinews* and *Penguins in Print* are not available in the U.S.A. or Canada

Karl Marx
Friedrich Engels

The Communist Manifesto

With an Introduction by A. J. P. Taylor

The complete text of the political tract which has
exercised so great an influence on the world in the past
century.

In a special introduction to this new edition A. J. P.
Taylor charts the progress of the *Manifesto* from
persecuted obscurity to global reverence and examines
the relevance of Marx's nineteenth-century ideas to
the realities of modern politics.

The Necessity of Art

A Marxist Approach

Ernst Fischer

On the first appearance in English of what is probably one of the most influential books on art to be published since the war, Kenneth Tynan wrote:

'In this challenging new Pelican Ernst Fischer, the Austrian poet and critic, surveys the whole history of artistic achievement through Marxist eyes.

People have always needed art: but why have they needed it? And what shaped the forms whereby they satisfied their need? Fischer's answers to these questions should be as voraciously studied and debated here as they have been on the Continent.

The book abounds in signs that Fischer is an empirical rather than a doctrinaire Marxist; you never feel he is tailoring his reactions to fit a thesis. 'A new art,' he says, 'does not come out of doctrines but out of works. Aristotle did not precede ... Homer, Hesiod, Aeschylus and Sophocles; he derived his aesthetic theories from them.'

Marxism has long needed an Aristotle; and in Ernst Fischer I suspect it has found its man.'

This book was first published in East Germany in 1959.